Make Poor Dad Rich Dad

Blueprint to Wealth, Success, and Financial Freedom

W J Francis

Copyright © 2024 by W J Francis
All rights reserved. No part of this book may be reproduced, distributed, or transmitted in any form or by any means, including photocopying, recording, or other electronic or mechanical methods, without the prior written permission of the publisher, except in the case of brief quotations embodied in critical reviews and certain other noncommercial uses permitted by copyright law.

DEDICATION

To the brilliant minds and tireless hands shaping the future of technology. Your innovation, perseverance, and passion power the world we live in today. This book is a tribute to your dedication in making the impossible, possible.

Disclaimer: The information contained in this book is for educational and informational purposes only. It is not intended as medical advice and should not be relied upon as such. The author and publisher are not responsible for any adverse effects or consequences resulting from the use of any information, suggestions, or recommendations in this book

Are you ready to rewrite the script of your financial destiny?

Make Poor Dad Rich Dad is more than just a book—it's a revolution in how you think about money, wealth, and success. This transformative guide unravels the secrets that separate those who struggle financially from those who thrive.

The Truth About Wealth: Discover why traditional money advice keeps you trapped and how to escape the cycle of financial mediocrity.

Two Daddies, Two Mindsets: Meet the "Poor Dad" who survives and the "Rich Dad" who thrives—and learn how to adopt the winning mindset.

Practical Blueprints for Success: From creating rock-solid financial goals to mastering money management, this book equips you with tools to take control of your finances.

The Power of Failures: Learn how to turn setbacks into stepping stones with the Failure Analysis Worksheet, designed to help you grow from every mistake.

A Lifetime of Wealth-Building Habits: Simple yet effective habits that guarantee long-term financial freedom.

Make Poor Dad Rich Dad isn't just another personal finance book—it's a game-changer for anyone ready to break free from financial limitations and live a life of purpose, wealth, and success.

If you've ever felt that wealth is reserved for "others," this book will shatter that myth and empower you to become the architect of your financial future.

Don't wait for success to find you—take action today and start your journey to becoming the "Rich Dad" in your own story.

W J Francis

CONTENTS

The Journey from Poor Dad to Rich Dad 9

Chapter 1: Understanding the Two Daddies 16

Chapter 2: Breaking Free from the Cycle of Poverty 34

Chapter 3: Building the Rich Dad Blueprint 53

Chapter 4: Mastering Money Management 73

Chapter 5: Earning the Rich Dad Way 92

Chapter 6: The Power of Financial Networking 114

Chapter 7: Investing Like Rich Dad 134

Chapter 8: Overcoming Setbacks and Failures 154

Chapter 9: Teaching the Next Generation 173

Chapter 10: The Rich Dad Mindset for Life 190

From Poor Dad to Rich Dad—Your Turn 209

The Journey from Poor Dad to Rich Dad

Life often presents us with moments of clarity, those instances when we realize the path we're on is unsustainable. For many, this realization comes in the form of financial stress—a mounting pile of bills, a lack of options, or the inability to say "yes" to the things that matter most. This is the story of transitioning from being a "Poor Dad," weighed down by financial burdens, to becoming a "Rich Dad," empowered and in control of your future.

The transformation isn't about luck or chance; it's about mindset, actions, and a commitment to creating lasting change. This journey isn't just about accumulating wealth; it's about redefining what wealth means for you and your family. Along the way, you'll discover tools, habits, and inspiration that can help you break free from financial fear and embrace a life of opportunity.

The "Poor Dad" Moment

For years, Mark worked tirelessly at his factory job. He prided himself on being a hard worker and a dependable provider for his wife and three children. Yet, despite the long hours, payday always seemed to come too late. He lived in a cycle of robbing Peter to pay Paul—credit cards maxed out, utility bills paid just in time to avoid disconnection, and barely enough left over for groceries.

The breaking point came during his son Jake's birthday. Jake had been asking for a new bicycle for months, and Mark had promised to make it happen. But as the day approached, he realized there was no way to afford it. Instead, he bought a small cake and hoped Jake wouldn't notice the missing gift.

But Jake did notice. That night, after the candles were blown out, Jake whispered, "It's okay, Dad. I know you're trying your best." Those words cut Mark deeper than any overdue notice. It wasn't just about the bike—it was about the life he was modeling for his children. He wanted to teach them to dream big, but his actions were teaching them to settle for less.

That evening, Mark made a decision that would change his life. He resolved to learn everything he could about managing money and building wealth, not just for himself but for his family.

The "Rich Daddy" Success Story

Fast forward ten years. Mark is now the proud owner of a successful landscaping business, earning more in a month than he used to in a year.

His family lives in a home they love, with savings in the bank and investments growing steadily.

But the greatest reward isn't the money—it's the freedom it has given his family. His daughter is studying abroad, his wife is pursuing her passion for painting, and Jake, now in college, often tells his dad, "You taught me how to dream, and you showed me how to make those dreams happen."

Mark's transformation wasn't magic. It was the result of consistent effort, learning, and a willingness to change. And it's a journey you can begin today.

Your Life with Financial Freedom

Imagine a life where money isn't a source of stress but a tool to achieve your goals.

Picture waking up each day with confidence, knowing that your bills are paid, your future is secure, and your family's dreams are within reach.

Think about the possibilities:

Taking your family on that dream vacation.

Starting a business you're passionate about.

Saying "yes" to your child's aspirations without hesitation.

Retiring early to spend more time with loved ones.

This life isn't a fantasy. It's achievable with the right mindset, tools, and actions. The journey begins with a single decision: the decision to change.

Reflection Prompts

Before diving into strategies, it's important to reflect on where you are and where you want to go. Take some time to answer these prompts honestly.

Writing your answers will help clarify your goals and identify the roadblocks you need to overcome.

1. What is your biggest financial fear?

Some common fears include:

Running out of money during retirement.

Being unable to provide for your children.

Remaining stuck in debt forever. By identifying your biggest fear, you can start addressing the root causes and find solutions.

2. What does "rich" mean to you?
For some, "rich" means financial freedom; for others, it's about having time and flexibility. Define what being "rich" means in your own life—this will serve as your guiding star.

3. What's one financial habit holding you back?

It might be impulse spending, neglecting to budget, or avoiding conversations about money. Recognizing these habits is the first step to replacing them with better ones.

4. Who inspires you to improve?

Identify someone—a mentor, a friend, or even a public figure—whose financial journey motivates you. What can you learn from their example?

The Journey to Rich Dad: Mindset Shifts

Becoming a Rich Dad isn't just about what you do—it's about how you think.

Here are three mindset shifts to embrace:

1. See Money as a Tool, Not a Burden

Money isn't inherently good or bad—it's a resource that can help you achieve your goals. Instead of fearing money, focus on learning how to manage and grow it.

2. Embrace a Growth Mindset

Your current financial situation doesn't define your future. With effort and education, you can change your circumstances and build the life you want.

3. Value Long-Term Gains Over Short-Term Gratification

Building wealth requires patience and discipline. Resist the temptation to prioritize instant gratification and focus on the bigger picture.

Actionable Steps to Transform Your Finances

Step 1: Assess Your Starting Point

Track Your Spending: Write down every expense for one month to identify areas where you can cut back.

Calculate Your Net Worth: Subtract your liabilities (debts) from your assets (savings, property, investments). This number will give you a baseline to measure your progress.

Step 2: Create a Budget

Allocate your income to essential expenses, savings, and discretionary spending.

Use the 50/30/20 rule as a guide: 50% for needs, 30% for wants, and 20% for savings and debt repayment.

Step 3: Build an Emergency Fund

Save 3–6 months' worth of living expenses to protect yourself from unexpected financial shocks.

Step 4: Eliminate Debt

Use the snowball method (paying off smallest debts first) or the avalanche method (tackling high-interest debts first).

Step 5: Invest in Your Future

Learn about investing through books, courses, or financial advisors.

Start small, even if it's just a few dollars a month. Compound interest is your best friend.

Make Poor Dad Rich Dad

Stories of Everyday Rich Daddies

The Side Hustler Kevin worked a 9-to-5 job that barely covered his expenses. He started a side hustle as a freelance graphic designer, working nights and weekends. Over time, his hustle grew into a full-time business, allowing him to quit his job and triple his income.

The Budgeting Master Sarah, a single mother, felt overwhelmed by her finances until she started using a simple app to track her spending. By sticking to her budget, she paid off $20,000 in debt in two years and began saving for her children's education.

The Ripple Effect

Your journey from Poor Dad to Rich Dad will have a profound impact on your family.

Here's how:

Empowering Your Children: Teaching financial literacy to your kids will set them up for success.

Strengthening Relationships: Financial security can reduce stress and strengthen bonds with your spouse and loved ones.

Creating a Legacy: The habits and wealth you build today will benefit future generations.

Final Reflection

Now that you've explored the principles and practices of becoming a Rich Dad, ask yourself:

What's the first step I can take today to change my financial future?

How will this journey impact my family's life in the next year? In the next decade?

The journey to financial freedom isn't a sprint—it's a marathon. But every step you take brings you closer to a life of possibility, abundance, and peace of mind.

It's time to rewrite your story. Your journey from Poor Dad to Rich Dad begins now.

Chapter 1: Understanding the Two Daddies

When we hear the phrase "Two Daddies," it evokes curiosity. Who are these two daddies? Are they real people or metaphorical representations? In this chapter, we delve into the concept of the "Poor Dad" and the "Rich Dad," exploring their contrasting mindsets, approaches to life, and influence on financial literacy.

The Foundation of Two Perspectives

The idea of the Two Daddies is rooted in the stark differences between poverty-driven and wealth-driven mentalities. "Poor Dad" symbolizes a traditional way of thinking, often shaped by scarcity, fear of risk, and adherence to conventional rules. "Rich Dad," on the other hand, embodies a growth-oriented mindset focused on opportunities, calculated risks, and innovation. These archetypes represent attitudes that influence not just financial outcomes but also personal growth, relationships, and decision-making.

Meet the Poor Dad

Poor Dad is not necessarily poor in monetary terms but in perspective. He prioritizes stability, security, and traditional paths to success.

For instance, Poor Dad might advise:

"Get a good education and secure a job with benefits."
"Save money and avoid debt at all costs."
"Play it safe; risks are for gamblers."

This perspective often stems from a fear of the unknown. It's shaped by societal expectations that equate stability with success. Poor Dad believes in working hard for others, climbing the corporate ladder, and eventually retiring with a pension. While this approach has its merits, especially in providing a sense of security, it can also limit opportunities for financial independence.

Characteristics of Poor Dad's Thinking

Fear of Failure: Avoidance of risks due to fear of loss.
Linear Growth Mindset: Belief that wealth accumulates slowly through diligent saving and controlled spending.
Dependency on External Systems: Reliance on employers, governments, or institutions for long-term stability.
Limited Financial Literacy: Focus on earning and saving but less emphasis on investing or wealth creation.

This mindset often perpetuates a cycle where wealth creation remains elusive. While the intentions are good, the results may not align with modern financial realities.

Enter the Rich Dad

Rich Dad represents a mindset shift. Instead of working for money, Rich Dad makes money work for him. This dad sees challenges as opportunities, prioritizes financial education, and values freedom over stability.

Rich Dad might say:

"Learn how money works before earning it."
"Take calculated risks to grow your wealth."
"Don't just save—invest wisely and diversify."

Rich Dad's focus is on building assets, reducing liabilities, and leveraging systems to generate passive income. This isn't about recklessness or blind ambition; it's about informed decision-making and understanding the principles of wealth generation.

Characteristics of Rich Dad's Thinking

Openness to Risks: Willingness to embrace uncertainty for long-term rewards.
Asset-Building Mentality: Focus on acquiring assets like real estate, stocks, businesses, or intellectual property.
Continuous Learning: Commitment to understanding markets, trends, and strategies.
Generational Wealth: Thinking beyond personal success and planning for future generations.

Rich Dad's approach empowers individuals to take control of their financial destiny rather than relying on others. It encourages creativity, resilience, and a proactive stance toward challenges.

The Emotional Connection

Understanding these two archetypes isn't just about money. It's about the emotional and psychological impact of their philosophies. Poor Dad's advice often comes from a place of love and protection, aiming to shield others from disappointment. Rich Dad, however, operates from a place of empowerment, pushing others to unlock their potential.

For example, Poor Dad might discourage a risky career move out of concern for stability, while Rich Dad would encourage it, seeing it as a stepping stone to growth. Both perspectives are valid in their contexts, but understanding when to apply each is critical.

Lessons from the Two Daddies

Balance Is Key: Both mindsets offer valuable insights. While Rich Dad encourages boldness, Poor Dad emphasizes caution. A balanced approach incorporates the best of both.

Learn from Experience: Both daddies represent lived experiences—use these lessons to craft your own path.

Define Your Success: Success looks different for everyone. Whether it's financial independence, personal fulfillment, or security, align your actions with your goals.

Building Bridges Between the Two

Adopting Rich Dad's mindset doesn't mean abandoning Poor Dad's values. Instead, it's about evolving traditional wisdom to meet contemporary needs.

For instance:

Combine Security with Growth: Save diligently but also explore investment opportunities.
Challenge Conventional Wisdom: Question norms that no longer serve you, like the idea that a single job guarantees lifelong security.
Embrace Lifelong Learning: Financial education doesn't end with school—it's an ongoing journey.

A Personal Reflection Exercise

To truly understand the Two Daddies, take a moment to reflect on your own experiences:

What financial advice have you followed in your life?
Which aspects align with Poor Dad's or Rich Dad's mindset?

How has this advice shaped your current financial situation?

By answering these questions, you can identify areas where a shift in mindset could lead to greater financial freedom.

Choosing Your Path

The journey from Poor Dad to Rich Dad isn't about rejecting one and embracing the other. It's about recognizing the strengths and limitations of each mindset and consciously choosing a path that aligns with your goals. By understanding these two archetypes, you can navigate the complexities of personal finance with clarity and confidence.

Perspective on Financial Mindsets

Once upon a time, in two corners of the world, lived two childhood friends who had taken very different paths in life. Amara, from Nairobi, Kenya, and Elias, from Stockholm, Sweden, had both grown up in modest families.

They shared dreams of a better future, but their financial choices and mindsets diverged as they matured, shaping their destinies in starkly contrasting ways. Their stories offer a global perspective on how financial attitudes can determine one's path in life.

Amara: A Story of Financial Scarcity

Amara grew up in a bustling Nairobi neighborhood where resources were limited, and financial knowledge was scarce. She had a sharp mind and big dreams, but her financial mindset was rooted in fear and scarcity—a perspective shaped by years of watching her parents juggle bills and emergencies without a safety net.

From a young age, Amara's family had always struggled with money. She often overheard her parents discuss debts and bills that seemed impossible to pay off. Despite their best efforts, there was never enough.

This financial environment shaped her view that money was something elusive, hard to keep, and easily lost.

When Amara graduated from college, she secured a stable government job in Nairobi. It was a position with security and benefits, and for Amara, that stability felt like the greatest achievement. However, the joy of stability soon faded.

Rather than investing in her future or saving, she spent the majority of her paycheck on immediate comforts. She bought the latest smart phone, treated herself to luxurious dinners, and even booked vacations to "live life to the fullest."

Amara told herself that she deserved these indulgences after years of hardship. She didn't consider the long-term implications of her financial choices. Instead of building wealth or even having an emergency fund, she thought of money as something to enjoy in the moment.

Then, one day, an unexpected medical expense arose. Without sufficient savings or insurance, she found herself in a tight spot. The cost was too much to bear, and she had to borrow money from friends and family.

The experience left her feeling both embarrassed and fearful. Still, she didn't change her habits. She continued living paycheck to paycheck, constantly running from one financial crisis to the next, just as her parents had before her.

Elias: A Mindset of Financial Abundance

Elias, on the other hand, grew up in Stockholm, where financial literacy was emphasized from a young age. His family wasn't wealthy, but his parents understood the value of savings, investment, and long-term financial planning.

Elias's father, an avid follower of Nobel laureate Muhammad Yunus's principles on microfinance, taught Elias the importance of viewing money as a tool for growth rather than mere consumption.

Make Poor Dad Rich Dad

While Elias didn't grow up wealthy, he learned to approach money strategically. At 16, he started a small online business reselling secondhand electronic gadgets. Instead of spending his earnings on video games or designer clothes like most of his peers, he saved a portion and reinvested the rest into expanding his business. Over time, he learned the value of making money work for him. Rather than thinking of money as something that would always slip away, he viewed it as a resource to help him build a future.

By the time Elias graduated college, his small business had grown into something far bigger. He used his savings to start a tech company, which would later take off and attract investors from around the world. While his friends from school were still searching for jobs, Elias had created a company that spanned continents, connecting Swedish technology with businesses in Asia and the Americas.

Elias was a firm believer in investing in himself. He often quoted Warren Buffett, one of the world's most successful investors, who once said, "Do not save what is left after spending, but spend what is left after saving." This idea drove Elias to prioritize investing over consumption.

Whether it was putting money into stocks, expanding his startup, or purchasing real estate, he chose options that generated passive income, understanding that wealth is not about immediate satisfaction, but about long-term growth.

Contrasting Financial Paths

Amara and Elias met again at their 10-year high school reunion. Their lives couldn't have been more different. Amara, though happy with her career, shared her struggles to stay financially afloat. She still lived in the same rented apartment and had little savings to her name. Her job was stable, but she admitted that financial emergencies constantly loomed over her like a dark cloud.

Elias, on the other hand, had become a well-traveled entrepreneur. His tech company was thriving, and he shared stories of his recent collaborations with international partners in Singapore and Canada.

Beyond financial success, he exuded confidence and freedom. Elias wasn't bound by financial stress because his wealth worked for him, not the other way around. He could afford to travel, invest further, and live a lifestyle that most people could only dream of.

Curious, Amara asked Elias how he had achieved so much. Elias explained, "It's about shifting your perspective. Money is a tool, not a goal. If you learn to invest and think ahead, you'll find opportunities instead of obstacles."

Elias told Amara about the various books he had read that shaped his mindset. From The Intelligent Investor by Benjamin Graham to Rich Dad Poor Dad by Robert Kiyosaki, he learned that financial independence wasn't about earning a higher salary—it was about changing how you used the money you already had.

A Global Financial Lesson

Amara and Elias's stories highlight a universal truth: financial mindset plays a pivotal role in shaping one's future. Across cultures, people like Amara focus on immediate gratification, often overlooking the long-term consequences of their spending habits. Conversely, individuals like Elias embrace a mindset of financial abundance, viewing money as a resource to create opportunities and freedom.

Around the world, renowned figures echo this wisdom. For instance, billionaire investor Ray Dalio from the United States emphasizes the importance of understanding financial systems to navigate life successfully. Dalio's book Principles: Life and Work underscores the need for discipline and strategic thinking in building wealth.

Similarly, Ratan Tata, one of India's most respected industrialists, advocates for investing in growth and innovation rather than short-term gains. His philanthropic ventures show how wealth can be used as a force for good, improving lives and fostering sustainable development. Tata has long been a proponent of using one's financial success to give back to society, believing that wealth, when earned with integrity, can be a tool for societal advancement.

In Japan, the concept of kaizen—continuous improvement—applies to finances as much as it does to personal and professional growth. This philosophy encourages small, consistent steps toward financial health, such as saving a percentage of income, investing for the future, or learning new skills to increase earning potential. It teaches that little improvements, compounded over time, can lead to great results.

Bridging the Gap: A Call to Action

Amara left the reunion inspired by Elias's journey and global examples of financial success. She realized that while her circumstances had shaped her mindset, she had the power to change it. Amara started by educating herself on financial literacy. She attended workshops, read books and began tracking her expenses to understand her spending habits.

Over time, Amara shifted her focus from consumption to creation. She launched a small side business making eco-friendly jewelry, reinvesting her profits to grow her venture. Though her progress was gradual, she felt empowered for the first time, knowing she was building a safety net and a brighter future.

The stories of Amara and Elias reflect a global narrative about financial mindsets. Across nations and cultures, the difference between financial struggle and success often lies in one's perspective on money. By adopting a mindset of growth and abundance, anyone can transform their financial reality.

As you reflect on this chapter, consider your financial mindset. Are you like Amara, focused on short-term comforts, or Elias, who sees money as a means to achieve long-term goals? Wherever you are on your financial journey, remember that the power to reshape your future lies within you. Start small, stay consistent, and watch as your wealth and opportunities grow—one thoughtful decision at a time.

The Motivational Journey to Mindset Mastery

Being "Poor Dad" isn't about how much money you earn or the wealth you currently have. It's about mindset—a perspective that can shape your choices, habits, and, ultimately, your future. The beauty of this concept is that it doesn't define anyone permanently. It emphasizes that you can transform into "Rich Dad" simply by changing how you think and approach life.

Breaking the Chains of the "Poor Dad" Mindset

The "Poor Dad" mindset stems from a belief system rooted in limitations. It's the voice that says, "I can't do this because I lack the resources" or "That opportunity isn't for people like me." This outlook isn't tied to a person's bank account but to their perception of what's possible.

This mindset traps people in a cycle of excuses, fear, and inaction. It's a learned behavior that often feels natural because it's influenced by upbringing, environment, and repeated experiences. But the first step to change is recognizing that these beliefs aren't truths—they're just stories we tell ourselves. And stories can be rewritten.

Shifting the Lens

Imagine putting on glasses with dark lenses. The world looks dim and constrained, regardless of how bright it actually is. The "Poor Dad" mindset works the same way—it filters life through a lens of scarcity. To move forward, you must swap those glasses for clear ones.

Make Poor Dad Rich Dad

A "Rich Dad" mindset is about seeing opportunities where others see obstacles. It's about believing that every problem has a solution, every failure is a lesson, and every setback is temporary. This isn't blind optimism; it's strategic thinking powered by self-belief.

Choosing Growth Over Comfort

One defining trait of the "Poor Dad" mindset is a preference for comfort over growth. It feels safer to stay in a familiar job, avoid risks, and live within the boundaries of what's known. But true growth requires stepping outside your comfort zone.

Think of growth like planting a seed. It's uncomfortable for the seed to break apart and push through the soil, but that process is necessary for it to bloom into a tree. Similarly, growth may feel challenging, but it's essential for transformation.

To shift into the "Rich Dad" mindset, embrace challenges as opportunities to stretch and learn. Say yes to situations that make you uncomfortable. Speak up in meetings, take a class on a topic that scares you, or pursue a side project you've been putting off. Growth is a choice you make daily.

Reframing Failure

One of the hallmarks of a "Poor Dad" mindset is a fear of failure. This fear paralyzes people into inaction, robbing them of the chance to succeed. But failure isn't the end—it's a stepping stone to success.

"Rich Dad" thinkers see failure as feedback. When something doesn't work, they ask themselves, "What can I learn from this?" rather than, "Why did this happen to me?" They recognize that every great success story is built on a foundation of setbacks.

By reframing failure as a teacher, you build resilience. The more you face failure, the less intimidating it becomes, and the closer you get to your goals.

Adopting an Abundance Mentality

The "Poor Dad" mindset often operates from a place of scarcity. It says, "If someone else wins, I lose." This creates envy, competition, and a reluctance to collaborate.

The "Rich Dad" mindset, on the other hand, embraces abundance. It understands that there's more than enough success to go around. When you celebrate others' achievements, you attract positivity into your life. Collaboration and networking become powerful tools to elevate everyone involved. Start small by shifting your language.

Instead of saying, "I can't afford this," try, "How can I afford this?" Instead of thinking, "This isn't possible," ask, "What steps can I take to make this possible?" Language shapes thought, and thought shapes action.

Cultivating Daily Habits

Mindset transformation doesn't happen overnight. It's built through consistent daily habits that reinforce new ways of thinking. Simple actions, repeated over time, lead to profound changes.

Start with these small yet powerful habits:

Gratitude Practice: Begin or end each day by listing three things you're grateful for. This trains your mind to focus on abundance rather than lack.
Positive Affirmations: Replace negative self-talk with empowering statements. For example, instead of saying, "I'll never be successful," say, "I am capable of achieving great things."
Continuous Learning: Read books, attend seminars, or listen to podcasts that inspire growth. Knowledge expands your perspective and opens doors to new opportunities.
Set Goals: Break your vision into small, actionable steps. Celebrate each milestone to build momentum.

Surround Yourself with Positivity: Spend time with people who uplift and inspire you. Distance yourself from negativity whenever possible.

The Power of Choice

Ultimately, the journey from "Poor Dad" to "Rich Dad" boils down to choice. Each day presents countless decisions that shape your future. Will you choose fear or courage? Scarcity or abundance? Excuses or action?

Recognize that you are not a victim of your circumstances. You are the author of your story. By taking responsibility for your mindset, you reclaim your power to create a life that aligns with your aspirations.

Inspiring Others

As you transform your own mindset, you naturally inspire those around you. Children, friends, and colleagues observe your actions and learn from your attitude. By embodying the "Rich Dad" mindset, you become a beacon of hope, proving that change is possible for anyone willing to try.

This ripple effect is perhaps the most rewarding part of the journey. Your success doesn't just benefit you—it empowers others to believe in themselves.

Being "Poor Dad" isn't a label—it's a mindset that can be changed. Your income, background, or current circumstances don't define your potential. What matters is your willingness to shift your perspective, embrace challenges, and take action.

The path to becoming "Rich Dad" isn't about accumulating wealth—it's about cultivating a mindset that attracts opportunities, fosters resilience, and celebrates growth.

It's about believing in your ability to create a better future and taking the steps to make it happen.

You hold the power to rewrite your story.

The question is: Are you ready to take the first step?

The journey to becoming financially independent often begins with understanding our habits, mindsets, and behaviors. Make Poor Dad Rich Dad offers actionable insights to transform a mindset of scarcity into one of abundance.

Below, we explore two practical tools designed to help you assess your current financial behaviors and reshape them to align with the practices of the "Rich Dad" mindset.

1. Behavior Chart: Spending vs. Saving, Scarcity vs. Growth Mindset

A critical first step in changing your financial future is recognizing the behaviors and thought patterns that guide your decisions. The following chart contrasts common habits of individuals operating under a "Poor Dad" mindset with those embracing the "Rich Dad" approach. By identifying where you currently stand, you can chart a path toward behaviors that lead to financial prosperity.

Behavior Comparison Chart

Aspect	Poor Dad (Scarcity Mindset)	Rich Dad (Growth Mindset)
Spending Habits	Spends impulsively without tracking.	Plans purchases, tracks expenses, and sets spending priorities.
Saving Habits	Views saving as restrictive or unnecessary.	Treats saving as a tool for future opportunities and security.
Income Perspective	Relies solely on active income (e.g., salary).	Creates multiple income streams (e.g., investments, side businesses).

Make Poor Dad Rich Dad

Aspect	Poor Dad (Scarcity Mindset)	Rich Dad (Growth Mindset)
Risk Attitude	Avoids risk out of fear of loss.	Takes calculated risks to grow wealth and learn from failures.
Education Priority	Thinks financial knowledge isn't important after school.	Continuously learns about investing, business, and personal finance.
Debt Management	Uses debt to finance liabilities like cars and gadgets.	Uses debt strategically to acquire assets that generate income.
Budgeting Approach	No consistent budgeting. Lives paycheck to paycheck.	Creates a realistic budget, prioritizing essentials and investments.
Problem-Solving	Focuses on why things can't be done.	Seeks creative solutions and thinks about *how* to achieve goals.
Generosity	Avoids giving, assuming there's never enough.	Gives strategically, believing in the abundance of resources.
Long-term Vision	Prefers instant gratification over long-term planning.	Delays gratification to focus on bigger, long-term rewards.

Reflection Exercise:
Identify one behavior in the "Poor Dad" column that you recognize in yourself.

Write down three steps you can take to move toward the corresponding behavior in the "Rich Dad" column.

2. Worksheet: "Which Dad Are You?"

This interactive worksheet helps you reflect on your current financial mindset and behaviors. By answering honestly, you can gain clarity on whether you lean more toward the "Poor Dad" or "Rich Dad" archetype.

Use this as a tool for self-awareness and a guide to develop a more prosperous mindset.

Instructions:

For each question, select the response that best describes your current habits or mindset. At the end, tally your results to see which mindset dominates your financial life.

Self-Assessment Questions

When you receive extra money (like a bonus or gift), what do you do first?

A) Spend it on something I've been wanting.
B) Set aside a portion for savings or investments.

How do you approach financial education?

A) I rarely think about learning more about personal finance.
B) I actively seek out books, podcasts, and courses to improve my financial knowledge.

When faced with a financial setback, how do you respond?

A) I feel defeated and blame external circumstances.
B) I analyze what went wrong and look for ways to bounce back.

Do you track your spending regularly?

A) No, I often lose track of where my money goes.
B) Yes, I review my spending and adjust my budget as needed.

What is your attitude toward debt?
A) Debt is just a part of life, and I don't think much about managing it.
B) I try to minimize unnecessary debt and use good debt to build assets.

How do you feel about taking financial risks?

A) I avoid risk because I'm afraid of losing money.
B) I take calculated risks, understanding that failure is part of the process.

What is your primary motivation for earning money?

A) To pay bills and enjoy life in the moment.
B) To build wealth and achieve financial freedom.

Do you have a long-term financial plan?

A) Not really; I focus more on immediate needs.
B) Yes, I have specific goals for savings, investments, and retirement.

Scoring and Analysis

For every A response, give yourself 1 point.
For every B response, give yourself 2 points.

Results:

8–12 points: You primarily align with the "Poor Dad" mindset. Start by focusing on small, achievable changes, such as tracking expenses or setting aside a fixed amount for savings.

13–15 points: You're transitioning toward a "Rich Dad" mindset, but there's room for growth. Work on strengthening your long-term planning and risk-taking strategies.

16 points: Congratulations! You're embracing the "Rich Dad" mindset. Keep refining your strategies to build even greater financial success.

How to Use These Tools

The chart and worksheet are not just about identifying problems—they're about creating a roadmap for change.

Here's how you can make the most of these tools:

Daily Awareness: Refer to the behavior chart regularly as a reminder of the habits you want to adopt.

Set Small Goals: Pick one behavior from the chart or worksheet each week and focus on improving it. For example, if you're not tracking expenses, start with a simple spreadsheet or app.

Accountability Partner: Share your results with a trusted friend or family member who can support your journey.

Track Progress: Revisit the worksheet every three months to assess how your mindset and habits have evolved.

By embracing these practical tools, you're taking the first steps to shift from a life of financial struggle to one of empowerment and growth.

Remember, change doesn't happen overnight. But with consistent effort and the right mindset, you can build a prosperous future and truly embody the lessons of Make Poor Dad Rich Dad.

Chapter 2: Breaking Free from the Cycle of Poverty

Breaking free from the cycle of poverty is one of the most transformative journeys a person or family can undertake. It's not just about escaping financial struggles—it's about reclaiming agency, embracing empowerment, and laying the foundation for a thriving future. Poverty is a complex challenge influenced by various factors such as lack of access to education, limited opportunities, systemic barriers, and personal circumstances. Yet, with the right mindset, strategies, and support systems, breaking this cycle becomes possible.

Understanding Poverty as a Cycle

Poverty often perpetuates itself through generations, creating a cycle that is difficult to escape. For example, a child born into a low-income family might lack access to quality education, leading to limited job opportunities later in life. With restricted earning potential, that individual may struggle to support their own children, who then face similar limitations.

This cycle is not just financial—it involves mental, emotional, and social constraints as well.

Recognizing poverty as a cycle helps us understand why it's not solely about working harder or cutting costs. It's about addressing the underlying causes and taking deliberate steps to disrupt this pattern.

Building the Right Mindset

Breaking the cycle starts with a shift in perspective. Often, poverty comes with feelings of helplessness and a belief that circumstances cannot change. Overcoming this mental barrier is crucial.

Adopt a Growth Mindset: A growth mindset means believing that abilities, intelligence, and circumstances can improve with effort and persistence. Instead of seeing challenges as permanent, view them as opportunities to grow and learn.

Set Clear Goals: Identify what you want to achieve. Whether it's financial independence, better education, or a stable job, having clear and specific goals gives you a direction to work toward.

Focus on Self-Worth: It's important to believe you are deserving of a better life. Self-worth fuels the motivation to pursue change and helps you push through obstacles.

Education as the Key to Freedom

Education is one of the most powerful tools to break the cycle of poverty. It opens doors to better job opportunities, higher earnings, and a broader understanding of the world.

Formal Education: For children, access to quality schooling is critical. Parents can prioritize their children's education, even in challenging circumstances, by seeking scholarships, affordable schooling options, or community support programs.

Lifelong Learning: For adults, the journey doesn't end with formal schooling. Learning new skills, attending workshops, or pursuing certifications can significantly improve employability and earning potential.

Financial Literacy: Many individuals trapped in poverty have limited knowledge about managing money. Learning about budgeting, saving, and investing can create pathways to financial stability and growth.

Financial Planning and Discipline
Managing limited resources effectively is a vital step in escaping poverty. This involves creating and sticking to a financial plan.

Create a Budget: Track your income and expenses to understand where your money is going. Allocate a portion for essentials, savings, and self-improvement.

Avoid Debt Traps: Many people in poverty fall into debt due to high-interest loans or credit card misuse. Prioritize paying off debts and avoid unnecessary borrowing.

Save Consistently: Even small amounts saved regularly can accumulate into a safety net. Establishing an emergency fund can prevent setbacks during unexpected challenges.

Explore Multiple Income Streams: Relying on a single source of income can be risky. Consider side gigs, freelance work, or small businesses to supplement earnings.

Building a Support Network

No one succeeds entirely alone. Having a strong support system can make a significant difference in breaking free from poverty. Seek Mentors: Find people who can guide you, share their experiences, and offer advice. Mentors provide encouragement and help you see possibilities you may not have considered.

Community Resources: Many communities have programs and organizations designed to help those in need. Take advantage of free workshops, job fairs, food banks, and housing assistance.

Surround Yourself with Positivity: The people you spend time with can influence your mindset and decisions. Build relationships with individuals who inspire, support, and challenge you to grow.

Overcoming Systemic Barriers

While individual actions are crucial, it's important to acknowledge that systemic issues also play a role in perpetuating poverty. Advocacy and community engagement can drive larger-scale change.

Participate in Local Initiatives: Volunteer or support programs that promote education, healthcare, and economic opportunities in your area.

Advocate for Policy Changes: Push for policies that ensure fair wages, affordable housing, and accessible education. Collective action can address barriers that no one person can overcome alone.

Collaborate with Others: Work with groups facing similar challenges. Together, you can amplify your voice and create more significant impact.

Cultivating Resilience

The journey out of poverty is rarely linear. Setbacks are inevitable, but resilience can keep you moving forward.

Learn from Failures: Every challenge carries a lesson. Reflect on setbacks, adjust your approach, and try again with greater insight.

Celebrate Small Wins: Acknowledge and appreciate progress, no matter how small. Each step forward builds momentum and confidence.

Stay Adaptable: Circumstances change, and being open to new opportunities or strategies can help you navigate unexpected situations.

Giving Back

Once you've made strides toward breaking free from poverty, consider helping others do the same.

Sharing knowledge, resources, and encouragement can create a ripple effect, uplifting entire communities.

Mentor Others: Share your story and offer guidance to those still struggling. Your experience can inspire others to believe in their potential.

Support Local Programs: Donate time, money, or skills to initiatives that aim to break the poverty cycle in your area.

Be a Role Model: By demonstrating what's possible, you can motivate others to pursue their goals and overcome challenges.

The Power of Hope and Determination

Breaking free from poverty requires hope—hope that circumstances can improve and that hard work will pay off. It also requires determination to persevere through challenges and make the most of every opportunity.

Every small step matters, from learning a new skill to saving a few dollars. With consistent effort, the cycle of poverty can be replaced with a cycle of opportunity, growth, and success. While the journey may be tough, the rewards—financial stability, self-fulfillment, and a brighter future for generations to come—are well worth the effort.

This transformation is not just about changing financial circumstances; it's about rewriting the story of your life and empowering others to do the same. The power to break free from poverty is within your grasp. It begins with believing in your potential and taking the first step forward.

Escaping Financial Struggles — Stories of Triumph

Financial hardship is a universal struggle, but stories of individuals who have broken free from the cycle of poverty provide hope and inspiration. In this chapter, we'll explore real-life accounts of people who transformed their lives, often against tremendous odds. These stories show that with determination, strategic action, and resilience, it is possible to escape financial struggles and create a secure future.

The Journey of Sara: From Minimum Wage to Entrepreneurial Success

Sara grew up in a small town where opportunities were scarce. She worked long hours as a cashier, earning just enough to scrape by. Despite her circumstances, she had a dream of running her own business. What made Sara's story remarkable was her ability to turn her vision into reality with limited resources.

At first, Sara spent her evenings learning about e-commerce through free online courses. She saved a small portion of her income, no matter how tight her budget was. Over time, Sara launched a small online store selling handmade jewelry, something she was passionate about.

The early days were challenging—her business made minimal profits, and she often second-guessed her decisions.

But Sara didn't give up. She reinvested her earnings to improve her products and marketing. With persistence, her store gained traction, and she started earning more than she ever had at her day job.

Within five years, Sara transitioned from working minimum wage to becoming a successful entrepreneur, employing others in her community. Her story reminds us that financial struggles are not permanent and can be overcome with creativity, learning, and perseverance.

Michael's Breakthrough: Conquering Debt and Building Wealth

Michael's financial troubles began with student loans and credit card debt. He followed the conventional path—getting a degree, finding a job, and assuming that life would naturally improve. But despite his efforts, Michael found himself drowning in debt by his early 30s. He felt stuck and hopeless.

One turning point came when he attended a free financial literacy seminar. For the first time, he understood concepts like budgeting, compound interest, and the impact of small, consistent investments. Motivated by this knowledge, Michael created a plan to tackle his debt.

He started by organizing his expenses, cutting unnecessary costs like dining out and subscriptions. Next, he picked up a side hustle as a freelance graphic designer, funneling all the extra income toward his highest-interest debts. Within three years, Michael paid off all his credit card debt.

But he didn't stop there. Michael began investing in index funds and real estate, slowly building wealth. A decade later, he not only escaped financial struggles but achieved financial independence. His story demonstrates the power of financial education and disciplined action in changing one's life trajectory.

Overcoming Systemic Barriers: The Story of Madam C.J. Walker

Madam C.J. Walker's story is one of the most inspiring examples of overcoming systemic barriers. Born in 1867 as Sarah Breedlove, she was the daughter of formerly enslaved parents and grew up during a time of extreme racial and gender discrimination.

Widowed at a young age and working as a laundress to support her daughter, Walker faced immense societal challenges.

Her turning point came when she began experimenting with hair care products for African American women, addressing a need that the mainstream beauty industry ignored.

Despite having little formal education and no financial safety net, she had an entrepreneurial spirit. Walker started selling her homemade products door-to-door and educating women about hair care.

Her business grew rapidly, and she eventually founded the Madam C.J. Walker Manufacturing Company. Through determination, innovation, and a deep understanding of her market, she became the first self-made female millionaire in America.

Walker's legacy is not just her wealth but her contributions to empowering women and breaking barriers in an unjust society.

Community Efforts That Sparked Change

Not all stories of escaping financial struggles are about individual triumphs. Sometimes, it takes a collective effort to uplift communities. In the early 2000s, a small farming village in India faced crushing poverty.

Most families relied on subsistence farming, earning barely enough to survive.

A group of women in the village formed a self-help group to pool their savings and offer small loans to one another. They began funding small projects, such as buying better seeds or starting micro-businesses.

With careful planning and mutual trust, their efforts bore fruit.

The group's success caught the attention of a local nonprofit, which provided them with training in sustainable farming and access to markets for their products.

Within a few years, the village's economy transformed. Families could afford education for their children, healthcare, and improved living conditions.

This story illustrates how collective action and support systems can empower individuals to escape financial struggles, even in the most challenging environments.

Breaking the Cycle: James and Intergenerational Wealth

James grew up in a household where money was always tight. His parents worked multiple jobs but never managed to save or invest. By the time James was in his early twenties, he realized he was on the same path.

Determined to change his family's financial story, he decided to break the cycle of paycheck-to-paycheck living.

James began by educating himself on personal finance. He set clear financial goals, such as saving for emergencies, paying off his car loan, and eventually buying a home. He started small, automating his savings and investing a portion of his income.

When James became a father, he prioritized teaching his children about money. He opened a savings account for his daughter's education and introduced her to basic financial concepts.

Over time, James built a modest but growing portfolio of investments.

Today, James's family is not only financially stable but also positioned to create intergenerational wealth. His story shows that breaking free from financial struggles isn't just about improving one's life—it's about creating a legacy for future generations.

The Role of Mindset in Overcoming Financial Struggles

These stories share a common thread: mindset. Financial struggles are often perpetuated by fear, lack of knowledge, or feelings of helplessness.

Each person in these stories adopted a mindset of growth, persistence, and learning.

Sara embraced the challenge of starting a business with limited resources. Michael transformed his fear of debt into motivation to learn and act. Madam C.J. Walker defied systemic barriers with unshakable determination.

The women in the Indian village believed in the power of community, and James decided to rewrite his family's narrative.

This mindset shift is not an instant solution but a foundational step. It allows individuals to see opportunities where others see obstacles, take calculated risks, and persevere despite setbacks.

Takeaways for Readers

Start Small: You don't need to have everything figured out to begin. Sara's story shows that even tiny steps, like saving a small amount or learning a new skill, can lead to big changes.

Educate Yourself: Financial literacy transformed Michael's life. There are countless free resources available today—books, podcasts, and online courses—that can help you make informed decisions.

Leverage Community: Whether it's a self-help group, a mentorship network, or simply a supportive circle of friends, having others to lean on can make a world of difference.

Break Barriers: Madam C.J. Walker's legacy reminds us that systemic challenges, while daunting, can be overcome with creativity and resilience.

Think Long-Term: Like James, think about how your financial decisions today can impact future generations.

Building wealth is not just about the present but also about creating a foundation for your family.

Financial struggles are a reality for many, but they don't have to be permanent. The stories here highlight the transformative power of determination, education, and action. They remind us that while the journey out of poverty is rarely easy, it is always possible. No matter where you start, there is always a way forward.

Reframe Poverty as a Starting Point, Not a Destiny

"Every setback is a setup for a comeback." This powerful quote encapsulates the essence of what it means to reframe poverty not as a lifelong limitation but as the beginning of a remarkable journey. Poverty, though challenging, is not the end of the road—it's the first chapter of a story waiting to unfold. When we shift our mindset, poverty transforms from an identity to a launch pad, from a prison to a platform.

The Narrative We Tell Ourselves

Imagine you're given a canvas smeared with smudges and stains. At first glance, it might seem ruined, but to an artist, it's a foundation for something beautiful. Poverty, too, can seem like a permanent flaw when viewed through the lens of despair. However, it becomes a foundation for growth when seen as an opportunity to create something extraordinary.

Many people grow up hearing phrases like, "We're just not lucky," or, "People like us don't succeed." These statements create mental walls that trap individuals in a cycle of self-limitation. But what if we rewrote that story? Instead of, "I come from nothing," the narrative becomes, "I come from somewhere that gave me everything I need to succeed—grit, resilience, and the hunger to do better."

Your starting point doesn't dictate your destination. It's merely a marker on the map. The road ahead, with all its twists and turns, is shaped by the choices you make and the determination you bring to the journey.

Poverty as a School, Not a Sentence

Consider poverty as a classroom. It teaches lessons that wealth might never offer. Resilience is born when every dollar is stretched to its maximum potential. Creativity flourishes when resources are scarce, and one must innovate to solve problems. Empathy deepens as you understand the struggles of others who share similar challenges.

Some of the most influential figures in history started from a place of lack. Oprah Winfrey grew up in rural poverty but leveraged her circumstances to cultivate a vision of a better future. Andrew Carnegie, the steel tycoon, was born into a poor family in Scotland and later remarked, "The man who acquires the ability to take full possession of his own mind may take possession of anything else to which he is justly entitled."

Each of these individuals learned from their circumstances rather than being defined by them. Poverty didn't hold them back—it prepared them for their ascent.

The Power of a Shifted Mindset

"Where you are is not who you are." This truth underscores the transformative power of mindset. Reframing poverty starts with understanding that financial struggle is a circumstance, not a character trait. It's not about ignoring the difficulties—it's about refusing to let them define you.

Instead of viewing poverty as a permanent scar, see it as a badge of honor—a reminder of where you started and what you've overcome. This perspective turns what feels like a disadvantage into an advantage. It fuels a determination to succeed, often stronger than those who have never faced hardship.

When you tell yourself, "This is temporary," you open the door to possibilities. A single belief can spark actions that lead to monumental change. That belief could be as simple as, "I can build something better."

Practical Steps to Reframe Poverty

Changing how you perceive poverty doesn't happen overnight. It requires deliberate steps to alter your mindset and actions.

Here are some strategies to help shift your perspective:

Focus on Gratitude
It might sound counterintuitive to practice gratitude in the face of financial struggle, but this practice can transform your outlook. Start by acknowledging the skills, relationships, and inner strengths you've developed because of your circumstances. Gratitude shifts your focus from what you lack to what you have, creating a foundation for growth.

Set Micro Goals
Grand dreams can feel overwhelming, especially when resources are limited. Break them into smaller, manageable steps. Each goal achieved becomes proof that progress is possible, reinforcing the belief that poverty is not your final destination.

Seek Role Models
Surround yourself with stories of people who rose from humble beginnings to achieve greatness. Their journeys serve as blueprints and inspiration. If they can do it, so can you.

Invest in Yourself
Education and self-improvement are the ultimate poverty disruptors. Whether it's reading books, attending free workshops, or acquiring skills online, each investment in your knowledge compounds over time.

Redefine Success
Success doesn't always mean material wealth. It can mean stability, relationships, personal growth, or the ability to give back. By expanding your definition of success, you create more opportunities to feel fulfilled and accomplished.

Poverty as Fuel for the Future

"Diamonds are made under pressure." This analogy is fitting for anyone who has experienced the weight of poverty. The pressures of limited resources, constant obstacles, and tough decisions don't break you—they shape you.

When you reframe poverty as a stepping stone, you start to see its hidden advantages. The perseverance developed in difficult times becomes your superpower in moments of opportunity. The adaptability honed by navigating uncertainty turns you into a problem-solver in ways others might not imagine.

Many entrepreneurs credit their humble beginnings for their tenacity and innovative thinking. Daymond John, founder of FUBU and investor on Shark Tank, often speaks about how growing up with limited means taught him resourcefulness and the value of hard work. In his words, "You don't need money to make money. You need a drive."

The Ripple Effect of Change

When you change your perception of poverty, you don't just transform your own life—you influence those around you. Family members, especially children, begin to see possibilities where they once saw barriers. Communities start to shift when individuals rise above their circumstances and lead by example.
One small step can trigger a domino effect. A parent who decides to go back to school inspires their child to pursue higher education. A neighbor who starts a small business motivates others to explore their entrepreneurial potential.

Dream Beyond the Struggle

Poverty has a way of shrinking dreams. It whispers, "That's not for people like you." But remember, every great achievement began with a dream. Don't let your circumstances limit your imagination.

Ask yourself, What would I do if I weren't afraid? Your answer to that question holds the key to your next step.

Dreaming beyond the struggle doesn't mean ignoring reality—it means believing that your reality can change.

Each small action you take in pursuit of that dream pulls you closer to a life of abundance and purpose.

The New Definition of Rich

The title Make Poor Dad Rich Dad isn't just about financial wealth—it's about richness in all aspects of life. Being "rich" means having meaningful relationships, a sense of purpose, and the freedom to live on your terms.

It's about thriving, not just surviving

When you reframe poverty, you begin to see richness in places you never expected.

The love of family, the value of community, and the strength within yourself become treasures that no monetary value can match.

A Call to Action

As you turn the page on this chapter of your life, ask yourself: How will I choose to view my starting point? Will it be a life sentence or the first step of an extraordinary journey?

You have the power to decide. Let poverty be the soil from which your dreams grow.

Let it teach you resilience, spark your creativity, and fuel your determination.

As you move forward, carry this truth: "Every setback is a setup for a comeback."

Identify One Belief About Money You Want to Unlearn

The Power of Beliefs About Money

Beliefs about money shape how we think, feel, and act in relation to wealth. These beliefs often stem from childhood experiences, cultural narratives, or personal encounters. While some money beliefs serve us well—encouraging saving, wise spending, or generosity—others can limit our potential. Unlearning unhelpful beliefs is key to creating financial freedom and abundance.

Let's dive into this transformational process with two practical tools: a journal prompt and a belief tracker worksheet.

Journal Prompt: Identifying One Limiting Money Belief

Reflecting on your thoughts and emotions is the first step to recognizing the beliefs holding you back. Below is a simple but powerful journal prompt designed to uncover one money belief that no longer serves you.

Prompt:
Think about your earliest memories of money. Who or what influenced your understanding of wealth? Write down one belief about money you've internalized that you now realize might be limiting. How has this belief impacted your financial decisions, career choices, or overall mindset?

Example Response:
"I've always believed, 'Money is the root of all evil.' I think this belief came from hearing it in my household growing up, where money was scarce, and wealthy people were often criticized. As a result, I've felt guilty about wanting to earn more, which has held me back from pursuing higher-paying opportunities. I'm starting to realize that money, in itself, is neutral—it's how people use it that determines its impact."

Your Turn: Take 10–15 minutes to respond to the prompt in your own words. Be honest and open; there are no right or wrong answers. Once you've written down your belief, you're ready to challenge and reframe it.

Challenging and Reframing the Belief

Now that you've identified a limiting belief, it's time to confront it.

Ask yourself:
Is this belief absolutely true?
What evidence contradicts it?
How would my life improve if I let go of this belief?

Example Reframe:
Limiting Belief: "Money is the root of all evil."
Reframe: "Money is a tool that can amplify goodness when used responsibly. It can fund dreams, support loved ones, and create positive change in the world."

The Role of a Belief Tracker

Shifting your mindset doesn't happen overnight. It's a gradual process that requires awareness and intentionality. A belief tracker worksheet is a practical tool to help you monitor your progress and stay committed to your journey.

Belief Tracker Worksheet

The belief tracker is divided into three sections:

Reflection on Current Beliefs
Tracking Mindset Shifts
Celebrating Progress

Here's how it works:

Section 1: Reflection on Current Beliefs

This section helps you record the limiting belief you're working to unlearn and your initial thoughts about it.

Use the following table format:

Limiting Belief	Impact on My Life	Desired New Belief
Money is the root of all evil.	I feel guilty for wanting to earn more, which holds me back from pursuing opportunities.	Money is a neutral tool that can create positive change.

Section 2: Tracking Mindset Shifts
Each week, take 5–10 minutes to reflect on how your mindset is evolving.

This section includes prompts such as:
What actions have I taken this week to challenge my belief?
What evidence have I noticed that supports my new belief?
How do I feel about money this week compared to last week?

Example Weekly Entry:

Date	Actions Taken	Evidence of New Belief	Feelings About Money
Week 1: Nov 27	Read an article about philanthropy by wealthy people.	Realized that money can fund education and health programs.	Feeling more optimistic about earning money.
Week 2: Dec 4	Budgeted for a small donation to a local charity.	Experienced the joy of giving back.	Feeling empowered and purposeful.

Section 3: Celebrating Progress
Tracking progress isn't just about identifying challenges—it's about celebrating wins. Use this section to document the positive changes you notice, no matter how small.

Prompts for Reflection:
What's one thing I did differently this week because of my new belief?
How has my relationship with money improved?

What financial goal feels more attainable now?

Example Entry:
"This week, I confidently negotiated a raise at work. I realized that earning more doesn't make me selfish; it gives me the ability to provide for my family and support causes I care about."

Integrating the Tools into Your Daily Life

Using the journal prompt and belief tracker together creates a powerful feedback loop. Start by journaling to uncover limiting beliefs, then use the belief tracker to guide your progress. Over time, these tools will help you replace limiting narratives with empowering ones.

Tips for Success:
Be Patient with Yourself: Changing deeply rooted beliefs takes time. Celebrate small victories along the way.

Stay Consistent: Dedicate a few minutes each week to update your belief tracker.

Seek Support: Share your journey with a trusted friend, mentor, or financial coach. Their encouragement can be invaluable.

A New Relationship with Money

By identifying and unlearning a limiting money belief, you're opening the door to a more abundant and fulfilling financial future. The process may feel challenging at times, but with tools like journaling and the belief tracker, you'll have the guidance and structure you need to succeed. Remember, your beliefs are not set in stone—you have the power to shape them and, in doing so, transform your life.

Now, grab a pen, start journaling, and begin your journey toward financial empowerment!

Chapter 3: Building the Rich Dad Blueprint

When we hear the term "Rich Dad," it's easy to conjure images of wealth, luxury, and financial freedom. But the essence of being a Rich Dad goes far beyond material wealth. It's about building a sustainable and holistic life that includes financial security, emotional well-being, and generational impact.

This chapter will guide you in constructing your personal Rich Dad Blueprint—a clear, actionable framework to transform your financial mindset and lifestyle.

1. Understand the Foundation: Financial Literacy

A solid blueprint starts with understanding the materials you're working with. In the case of building wealth, financial literacy is your foundation. It involves knowing how money works, how it grows, and how to protect it.

To develop financial literacy:

Educate Yourself: Begin with basic concepts like budgeting, saving, and investing. Learn about compound interest, inflation, and debt management.

Track Your Money: Create a habit of monitoring income and expenses. Use tools like apps or spreadsheets to make this process easier.

Understand Financial Systems: Dive into topics like taxes, credit scores, and economic trends. The more you know, the better decisions you'll make.

2. Adopt the Rich Dad Mindset

Your mindset shapes your financial future. A Rich Dad sees opportunities where others see obstacles, and values long-term gain over short-term gratification.

Here's how to cultivate this mindset:

Embrace Delayed Gratification: Resist the urge for instant rewards. Instead, focus on investments or decisions that yield long-term benefits.

Learn from Failures: View mistakes as lessons, not roadblocks. Every failure brings insight that can lead to success.

Visualize Abundance: Train your mind to believe in endless possibilities. Rich Daddies don't operate from a scarcity mindset—they think expansively.

3. Master the Art of Earning

While saving and investing are crucial, building wealth begins with earning. Diversifying income streams is key to financial independence.

Identify Your Skills and Strengths: Assess what you're good at and how you can monetize it. This could mean pursuing a higher-paying job, freelancing, or starting a business.

Invest in Yourself: Take courses, read books, and acquire new skills. Continuous learning increases your value in the marketplace.

Explore Passive Income Opportunities: Real estate, dividend stocks, royalties, or creating digital products are excellent ways to earn while you sleep.

4. Save Smart, Not Just Save More

Saving is essential, but it's equally important to save with intention. Mindless saving can lead to missed investment opportunities.

Automate Your Savings: Set up automatic transfers to savings accounts to build discipline effortlessly.

Establish an Emergency Fund: Aim for 3–6 months of living expenses to cover unexpected events.

Prioritize High-Yield Accounts: Look for savings accounts or investment vehicles that offer competitive returns.

5. Invest Wisely to Build Wealth

Investing is where your money begins to work for you. A Rich Dad knows the power of smart investments to generate wealth over time.

Start Early: Time is the greatest ally for investments, thanks to compound growth. Begin as soon as possible, even with small amounts.

Diversify: Avoid putting all your money into one asset. Spread investments across stocks, bonds, real estate, and other opportunities.

Stay Informed: Research market trends and understand the risks involved. Investing without knowledge is gambling.

6. Master Budgeting and Cash Flow Management

Budgeting is the backbone of the Rich Dad Blueprint. Without a clear understanding of cash flow, wealth can slip through your fingers.

Categorize Expenses: Divide expenses into needs, wants, and luxuries. Prioritize needs, moderate wants, and limit luxuries.

Create a Zero-Based Budget: Allocate every dollar of income to a specific purpose, ensuring no money is unaccounted for.

Review Regularly: Adjust your budget as your circumstances change to stay on track.

7. Build and Protect Your Legacy

Being a Rich Dad isn't just about personal wealth; it's about creating a legacy for future generations.

Teach Financial Responsibility: Share your knowledge with your children or younger family members to ensure they continue your wealth-building principles.

Create a Will and Estate Plan: Ensure your assets are distributed according to your wishes. Seek professional advice if needed.

Invest in Relationships: Wealth is not just monetary. Strong relationships with family, friends, and mentors provide invaluable support and wisdom.

8. Embrace Smart Debt Management

Debt isn't always bad—it's how you use it that matters. Rich Daddies understand the difference between good and bad debt.

Good Debt: Loans or credit that generate income, like mortgages for rental properties or education loans that enhance your earning potential.

Bad Debt: High-interest credit card balances or loans for depreciating assets. Avoid these wherever possible.

Develop a Repayment Strategy: Focus on paying off high-interest debts first while keeping manageable payments on lower-interest ones.

9. Surround Yourself with Success

The people you associate with influence your financial habits and outlook. Surround yourself with individuals who share your aspirations and values.

Seek Mentors: Learn from those who have already achieved financial success.

Build a Supportive Network: Engage with like-minded peers who can offer encouragement, advice, and accountability.

Avoid Toxic Influences: Distance yourself from individuals who discourage your goals or promote reckless financial behavior.

10. Practice Generosity and Gratitude

A Rich Dad recognizes that wealth is not just about accumulation but also about impact. Giving back enriches your life and inspires others.

Donate to Causes You Believe In:

Support charities or initiatives that align with your values.

Volunteer Your Time: Contributing time is as valuable as contributing money.

Cultivate Gratitude: Acknowledge what you have achieved and appreciate the journey.

Gratitude fosters a positive mindset and attracts abundance.

11. Stay Committed and Consistent

Building wealth isn't a one-time effort; it's a lifelong commitment.

Set Clear Goals: Define what wealth means to you—whether it's early retirement, a dream home, or financial security for your children.

Track Progress: Regularly review your financial goals and adjust strategies as needed.

Stay Resilient: Financial journeys come with challenges. Learn to adapt and persevere.

12. Innovate and Adapt to Change

The financial landscape is constantly evolving. To stay ahead, you must be willing to innovate and adapt.

Embrace Technology: Use financial apps and tools to streamline budgeting, investing, and tracking expenses.

Keep Learning: Stay updated on market trends, new investment opportunities, and emerging technologies.

Be Open to Change: As your life circumstances change, so should your financial plans. Flexibility is crucial for success.

The Rich Dad Blueprint is not a one-size-fits-all model. It's a personalized, dynamic approach that reflects your goals, values, and vision for the future. By focusing on financial literacy, cultivating the right mindset, and making intentional decisions, you can turn your dreams of financial independence into reality.

This journey is about more than money; it's about creating a life of purpose, security, and lasting impact. Start building your blueprint today—your future self and generations to come will thank you

A Journey from Financial Struggle to Success
The Story of Sarah Parker

Sarah Parker's story is an inspiring tale of resilience, resourcefulness, and the transformative power of understanding basic financial principles. Born into a modest household, Sarah grew up in a small town where financial literacy wasn't a priority. Her parents, though hardworking and loving, often struggled to make ends meet. By the time Sarah graduated college, she carried not only a diploma but also $40,000 in student loans and credit card debt from years of living beyond her means.

The Breaking Point

At 27, Sarah hit rock bottom. She was working a retail job with little room for growth, living paycheck to paycheck, and overwhelmed by her mounting debt. Then came a day she would never forget: her car broke down, and she didn't have the funds to repair it. Forced to walk miles to and from work, Sarah realized she could no longer ignore her financial situation. Something had to change.

"I didn't want to live this way anymore," Sarah recalls. "I was tired of feeling stuck and powerless. That's when I decided to educate myself about money."

The Turning Point: Learning Basic Financial Principles

With determination in her heart and just $50 in her savings account, Sarah turned to the library.

She began reading books and watching videos on financial literacy.

The more she learned, the more she realized how simple yet effective financial principles could be.

The first principle she embraced was budgeting.

Using the 50/30/20 rule, she allocated her income into three categories:

50% for needs: Rent, groceries, utilities.
30% for wants: Small indulgences like an occasional coffee or streaming subscriptions.
20% for savings and debt repayment: Aggressively tackling her loans while building an emergency fund.

For the first time, Sarah had clarity about where her money was going.

The Power of Mindset Shift

Another principle Sarah adopted was shifting her mindset about money. Instead of viewing it as something scarce or stressful, she began seeing it as a tool to achieve her goals.

She started tracking her spending daily, which not only helped her control unnecessary expenses but also gave her a sense of accomplishment.

"I realized I had to stop comparing myself to others. I didn't need the latest phone or expensive clothes to feel good about myself. What I needed was financial freedom," Sarah says.

Side Hustles and Additional Income

Realizing that her retail job alone wouldn't suffice, Sarah explored ways to increase her income. She turned a hobby into a side hustle, selling handmade jewelry online.

Though the initial income was modest, it grew steadily over time.

In addition, Sarah took up freelance writing, leveraging her degree in English. Every extra dollar she earned went toward paying down her debts. She also worked weekends at a local farmer's market, further accelerating her progress.

Smart Debt Repayment Strategies

Sarah discovered the debt snowball method, which involves paying off the smallest debt first while making minimum payments on the rest.

With each small victory, she gained confidence and momentum.

"Paying off my first credit card balance of $500 felt amazing," Sarah remembers. "It made me believe I could tackle the bigger debts too."

Over the next two years, Sarah eliminated all her credit card debt and made significant progress on her student loans.

Building an Emergency Fund

Once her debt was under control, Sarah focused on building an emergency fund. She started with a goal of saving $1,000 and eventually expanded it to cover three months' worth of living expenses.

This financial cushion gave her peace of mind and the freedom to make better decisions.

Investing for the Future

Sarah's newfound financial literacy didn't stop at budgeting and debt repayment. She wanted to secure her future and began exploring investment opportunities.

Starting small, she opened a Roth IRA and invested in low-cost index funds. The power of compound interest amazed her.

"Knowing that my money was working for me, even while I slept, was empowering," Sarah says.

Make Poor Dad Rich Dad

Teaching Others

As Sarah's financial situation improved, she became passionate about helping others. She started a blog where she shared practical tips and personal anecdotes about her journey. Her authenticity resonated with readers, and the blog became a source of supplemental income.

Sarah also volunteered to teach basic financial principles at a local community center, empowering others to take control of their finances.

The Results

By the time Sarah turned 35, she was debt-free, had a healthy emergency fund, and was on track to retire early. She had transitioned from her retail job to a fulfilling career in marketing, thanks to the skills and confidence she gained during her financial transformation.

"I'm not a millionaire," Sarah says. "But I'm rich in ways that matter. I have control over my life, the freedom to pursue my dreams, and the ability to help others. That's true wealth."

Lessons from Sarah's Journey

Sarah's story underscores several key lessons that anyone can apply:

Start Where You Are: No matter how dire your financial situation, small changes can lead to big results over time.

Educate Yourself: Knowledge is power. Understanding basic financial principles is the first step toward empowerment.

Budgeting is Essential: A budget isn't restrictive—it's a roadmap to achieving your goals.

Focus on Mindset: A positive outlook and clear priorities are critical for long-term success.

Diversify Your Income: Side hustles and additional streams of income can accelerate progress.

Celebrate Small Wins: Each milestone, no matter how small, builds confidence and momentum.

Pay It Forward: Sharing what you've learned can inspire and uplift others.

Sarah Parker's journey from financial struggle to stability is a testament to the power of basic financial principles. It's a story of hope, resilience, and the belief that change is possible with knowledge and determination. Her success reminds us that while wealth isn't always about the numbers in your bank account, it's always about the choices you make.

For anyone feeling overwhelmed by their finances, Sarah's advice is simple: "Take one step today. Open a book, track your spending, start saving—even if it's just $5. Those small actions will compound into something extraordinary over time."

The Simplicity and Power of Taking Small, Consistent Steps

We often dream of transforming our lives, building wealth, and achieving freedom. Yet, many of us find ourselves paralyzed, unsure where to begin.

This hesitation often stems from the misconception that change requires monumental, immediate actions.

However, the truth is quite the opposite: the most profound transformations come from small, consistent steps taken every day. This principle, simple yet powerful, is the cornerstone of the "Rich Dad Blueprint."

Why Small Steps Matter

Small steps are achievable, manageable, and sustainable. Imagine trying to climb a mountain in a single leap. It's impossible, exhausting, and discouraging. Now imagine breaking that climb into tiny steps, focusing only on the next foothold. Each step builds momentum, and before you know it, you're at the peak.

The same principle applies to building wealth and reshaping your financial future. A single dollar saved today may seem insignificant, but over time, it can grow into a substantial sum when paired with discipline and strategic investment. A single skill you learn today may not change your life overnight, but it becomes a tool you can leverage for years to come.

Small steps compound over time, creating exponential growth. This is the magic of consistency. It transforms the ordinary into the extraordinary, like water dripping persistently on stone until it carves a path.

Breaking the Myth of Overnight Success

We live in a world obsessed with instant gratification. Social media bombards us with success stories that seem to happen overnight—a young entrepreneur creates a startup and suddenly becomes a millionaire, or an investor hits the jackpot with one lucky trade.

What these stories rarely show are the years of preparation, learning, and small, consistent steps that led to those "overnight" successes.

The Rich Dad Blueprint does not promise shortcuts or miracles. Instead, it offers a roadmap grounded in reality. It's about creating a vision for your financial future and breaking it into actionable, manageable steps. The power lies in simplicity and consistency.

The Power of Habits

At the heart of taking small, consistent steps is the development of habits. Habits shape our daily lives, guiding our decisions almost automatically. Imagine if you could program yourself with habits that naturally lead to financial success. This is entirely possible by starting small.

Here's how it works:

Identify One Tiny Change: Start with one habit that aligns with your financial goals. For example, commit to saving $5 a day or reading five pages of a personal finance book each evening.

Anchor the Habit: Tie the new habit to an existing one. For instance, if you have a morning coffee routine, use that time to review your spending from the previous day.

Celebrate Small Wins: Each time you complete your small step, acknowledge the accomplishment. Small celebrations reinforce the behavior and make it enjoyable.

Over time, these habits become automatic. Saving $5 a day evolves into saving $150 a month. Reading five pages a night leads to 1,825 pages a year—the equivalent of about nine books. These small, consistent actions create a foundation for success.

Envisioning Your Rich Dad Blueprint

Before taking steps, you need a clear destination. This is where envisioning your Rich Dad Blueprint comes into play.

A blueprint is a detailed plan that outlines the structure of a building before it's constructed.

Similarly, your Rich Dad Blueprint is a vision of your ideal financial life, broken into actionable components.

Make Poor Dad Rich Dad

Here's how to create your Rich Dad Blueprint:

Define Your Why: Why do you want to build wealth? Your "why" gives purpose to your journey. It could be to provide a better future for your family, achieve financial independence, or leave a legacy.

Picture Your Ideal Life: Visualize your "rich" life in vivid detail. What does your day look like? Where do you live? How do you spend your time? Be specific.

Set Tangible Goals: Break down your vision into measurable, time-bound goals.

For instance:

Save $10,000 in an emergency fund within two years.
Pay off $20,000 in debt over five years.
Invest $500 monthly to build a retirement fund.

Map the Journey: Identify the small, consistent steps needed to reach these goals. If your goal is to save $10,000, the first step might be opening a dedicated savings account and automating a monthly deposit.

Examples of Small Steps with Big Impact

The Dollar-A-Day Habit: Saving just one dollar a day may seem trivial, but over a year, it adds up to $365.

With interest or investment, this small habit can grow significantly over time.

Learning One New Skill: Commit to learning a new skill that increases your earning potential, such as coding, graphic design, or sales.

Dedicate 15 minutes a day to practice, and within a few months, you could open doors to new opportunities.

Tracking Expenses: Spend five minutes daily reviewing your spending.

This awareness can reveal patterns, helping you cut unnecessary expenses and redirect funds toward savings or investments.

Building a Network: Reach out to one person a week who inspires you or works in a field you admire.

Over a year, you'll have 52 connections, any of which could lead to mentorship, partnerships, or new opportunities.

Staying Motivated on the Journey

The path to wealth is a marathon, not a sprint.

Here's how to stay motivated as you take small steps:

Keep Your Blueprint Visible: Place a visual representation of your goals somewhere you see daily.

It could be a vision board, a list of milestones, or a simple sticky note with your "why."

Track Progress: Celebrate each milestone, no matter how small. Tracking progress shows how far you've come and fuels your desire to keep going.

Embrace Setbacks: Understand that setbacks are part of the journey. Learn from them, adjust your strategy, and keep moving forward.

Seek Support: Share your goals with supportive friends or join a community of like-minded individuals.

Encouragement and accountability make the journey easier and more enjoyable.

The Ripple Effect of Consistency

The beauty of small, consistent steps is that they create a ripple effect. The discipline and habits you develop in one area of your life often spill into others. Saving money can lead to healthier spending habits. Learning a new skill can boost your confidence and open doors in your career. These ripples expand, amplifying your progress and creating a life that reflects the Rich Dad Blueprint.

The simplicity of small, consistent steps is both empowering and liberating. It shifts the focus from daunting transformations to manageable actions you can take today. Every step, no matter how small, brings you closer to your vision.

The journey to becoming a "Rich Dad" starts with a single decision: to take the first step. As you continue, those steps will multiply, creating a life of abundance, freedom, and purpose. So take a moment to reflect, envision your blueprint, and start building your future one small step at a time. Your Rich Dad life awaits.

Template for Drafting Personal Financial Goals and a Checklist

Creating a roadmap for personal financial success begins with two essential components: a well-crafted financial goals template and a reliable checklist of foundational financial habits. Let's explore how to build these tools in a way that is practical, actionable, and adaptable.

A Template for Drafting Personal Financial Goals

Define Your "Why"

Every financial goal should have a purpose that resonates with your values. Are you saving for your child's education, a dream vacation, or an early retirement? Start by writing a short statement for each goal that captures why it matters to you.

Example:

Goal: Save $50,000 for a house down payment.
Why: To provide a secure and stable home for my family.
Set SMART Goals.
SMART stands for Specific, Measurable, Achievable, Relevant, and Time-bound.

Ensure your goals tick all these boxes:

Specific: Clearly state the amount or milestone.
Measurable: Track your progress with precise numbers.
Achievable: Ensure it's realistic within your resources.
Relevant: Align it with your overall life aspirations.
Time-bound: Assign a deadline to create urgency.

Example Template:

Specific: Save $20,000.
Measurable: Deposit $500 monthly into a high-yield savings account.
Achievable: Reduce non-essential expenses to meet the target.
Relevant: Build a safety net for emergencies.
Time-bound: Achieve this in three years.

Prioritize Your Goals

List all your financial goals and rank them based on urgency, importance, and feasibility.
Short-term (less than 1 year): Emergency fund, clearing small debts.
Medium-term (1–5 years): Saving for a car, wedding, or business capital.
Long-term (5+ years): Retirement, children's education.

Break It Down
Large goals can feel overwhelming. Break them into smaller, actionable steps.

Make Poor Dad Rich Dad

For example:

Goal: Save $10,000 for a car.
Monthly Savings Target: $500.
Weekly Action: Track expenses and cut $125 in discretionary spending.

Accountability and Adjustment

Use tools like budgeting apps, spreadsheets, or even a simple notebook to monitor your progress. Schedule monthly check-ins with yourself or a trusted partner to review and adjust as needed.

Visualize Success

Keep your goals in sight. Create a vision board, or use sticky notes to remind yourself of what you're working toward. Visualization fosters motivation and commitment.

A Checklist of Foundational Financial Habits

Strong financial habits are the backbone of achieving your goals.

Incorporate the following practices into your daily, weekly, and monthly routines:

1. Know Your Numbers
Track Income and Expenses: Maintain a monthly budget.
Understand Your Net Worth: Calculate your assets minus liabilities quarterly.
Quick Tip: Use apps like Mint or YNAB to simplify tracking.

2. Build an Emergency Fund
Aim to save 3–6 months' worth of essential expenses. Begin by allocating even small amounts consistently.
Example:
Weekly Savings Goal: $20.
Deposit into: A separate, easily accessible savings account.

3. Pay Yourself First
Treat savings like a mandatory bill. Automate transfers to your savings account immediately after payday. Why It Works: It reduces the temptation to spend first and saves whatever is left (usually nothing).

4. Live Below Your Means
Resist lifestyle inflation as your income grows. Always find ways to cut unnecessary spending.
Tips:
Cook meals at home instead of eating out.
Opt for second-hand purchases where possible.

5. Eliminate Debt
Focus on high-interest debts first using methods like the avalanche or snowball strategy.
Avoid accumulating new debt unless it's strategic (e.g., student loans, home loans).

Checklist for Debt Management:

Create a repayment plan.
Negotiate better terms with lenders.
Celebrate small wins, like paying off a single credit card.

6. Protect Your Finances
Insurance: Ensure adequate coverage for health, life, home, and auto.
Emergency Plans: Have a will and designate beneficiaries.
Digital Security: Protect financial accounts with strong passwords and two-factor authentication.

7. Invest Wisely
Start early to take advantage of compound interest.
Diversify your portfolio across assets like stocks, bonds, real estate, and mutual funds. Consult a financial advisor if unsure.

8. Continuously Educate Yourself
Read books, listen to podcasts, or follow experts in personal finance. Stay updated on financial trends and tools.

9. Review Regularly
Financial situations evolve. Set a schedule to reassess your budget, goals, and habits every quarter.

10. Celebrate Wins
Acknowledge milestones, whether it's paying off a loan or saving your first $1,000. Rewards (small and within budget) reinforce positive habits.

Drafting personal financial goals and building foundational habits are two sides of the same coin. The template guides you on what to achieve, while the checklist ensures you build the discipline needed to succeed.

Start small, stay consistent, and keep adapting your approach. With these tools, you can transform your financial life step by step, turning aspirations into tangible achievements.

Chapter 4: Mastering Money Management

Money management is not just a skill; it's a mindset—a tool to create the life you envision for yourself and your family. Mastering money is about making deliberate, informed decisions that align with your goals and values.

Think of it as learning to drive a car. Without guidance, you might find yourself stalled or headed in the wrong direction. With a roadmap, however, you can confidently navigate to your destination.

Understanding the Basics of Money

Before mastering money management, it's important to understand what money represents. Money is a medium of exchange that measures the value of goods and services. It's not inherently good or bad—it's a resource.

By shifting your mindset from seeing money as a source of stress to seeing it as a tool for empowerment, you set the stage for financial mastery.

Consider this: every dollar you earn and spend is a reflection of your priorities. If you don't consciously decide where your money goes, you'll find it slipping through your fingers on things that don't matter.

Step 1: Assess Your Financial Reality

You cannot manage what you don't measure. Start by assessing your current financial situation.

This involves three simple steps:

Track Your Income: Understand how much money comes in every month. Include all sources—your salary, business income, side gigs, and passive earnings.

Monitor Your Expenses: Write down every expense for at least a month, from bills and groceries to coffee runs and subscriptions. This exercise often reveals surprising patterns.

Calculate Your Net Worth: Subtract your liabilities (debts) from your assets (savings, investments, and property). This number provides a snapshot of your financial health.

Awareness is power. By knowing where you stand, you can plan effectively.

Step 2: Set Clear Financial Goals

Money management without goals is like wandering in a desert without a compass. Financial goals give your money a purpose and direction.

Break your goals into three categories:

Short-Term Goals: These are goals you aim to achieve within a year, such as paying off a credit card, building an emergency fund, or saving for a vacation.

Mid-Term Goals: These span one to five years, like saving for a down payment on a house, buying a car, or starting a business.
Long-Term Goals: These may take over five years and include milestones like retirement savings, funding your child's education, or purchasing property.

Make your goals SMART—specific, measurable, achievable, relevant, and time-bound. For example, instead of saying, "I want to save money," set a goal like, "I will save $10,000 for a down payment within two years by saving $417 per month."

Step 3: Create a Budget That Works

Budgeting is the cornerstone of money management. A budget isn't about restricting your spending; it's about ensuring your money goes where it matters most.

Start with the 50/30/20 rule as a guide:

50% for Needs: Essential expenses like housing, utilities, groceries, and transportation.
30% for Wants: Non-essential but enjoyable expenses, such as dining out, entertainment, and hobbies.
20% for Savings and Debt Repayment: Building your emergency fund, investing, and paying off debts.
Adapt this framework to fit your unique circumstances. The goal is to create a system that is realistic and sustainable.

Step 4: Build an Emergency Fund

An emergency fund acts as a financial safety net, shielding you from life's unexpected challenges, such as medical expenses, car repairs, or job loss. Aim to save at least three to six months' worth of living expenses.

Start small if needed. Even setting aside $500 can make a difference. Automate your savings by setting up a direct deposit into a separate account to make it easier to grow your fund over time.

Step 5: Manage Debt Strategically

Debt can feel like a weight holding you back, but not all debt is bad. The key is to manage it wisely.

Divide your debt into two categories:

Good Debt: Debt that helps you build assets or grow wealth, such as student loans, mortgages, or business loans.

Bad Debt: Debt that doesn't offer long-term value, like high-interest credit card balances or payday loans.

Use the snowball method (paying off the smallest debt first for quick wins) or the avalanche method (tackling the highest-interest debt first to save on interest).

Choose the strategy that motivates you the most and stay consistent.

Step 6: Embrace Smart Saving and Investing

Saving money is the foundation, but investing is where wealth grows. Start with small, regular contributions to your savings account or retirement fund. Compound interest will do the heavy lifting over time.

When ready, explore investment options such as stocks, bonds, mutual funds, or real estate. Educate yourself and consider seeking advice from a financial advisor.

Remember, investing involves risk, so diversify your portfolio to reduce potential losses.

Step 7: Protect Your Wealth

As you grow your wealth, protecting it becomes essential.

This includes:

Insurance: Ensure you have adequate coverage for health, life, property, and liability.

Estate Planning: Create a will to define how your assets should be distributed.

Fraud Prevention: Monitor your accounts regularly and use strong passwords to guard against identity theft.

Step 8: Develop Strong Money Habits

Good money management is not about occasional big moves—it's about consistent habits.

Incorporate these practices into your routine:

Automate Savings and Bills: Reduce the risk of missed payments and make saving effortless.

Live Below Your Means: Spend less than you earn, no matter your income level.

Educate Yourself: Continuously learn about personal finance through books, podcasts, or courses.

Review Your Budget: Revisit your budget monthly to ensure it aligns with your goals and circumstances.

Step 9: Stay Motivated and Accountable

Financial management can be a long journey, so staying motivated is key. Celebrate milestones, no matter how small, and remind yourself why you started.

Share your goals with a trusted friend or family member who can keep you accountable.

Mastering money management is about progress, not perfection. It's a journey of empowerment, where each step brings you closer to financial freedom and security.

By taking charge of your money, you're not just changing your finances—you're transforming your life and setting an example for those around you.

Remember, every dollar is a building block. Use it wisely, and watch your vision of prosperity come to life.

Tale About Poor Money Management Leading to Financial Stress

Money has the power to create both security and stress, depending on how it is managed. A single misstep can lead to a cascade of financial challenges, creating a scenario where financial stress becomes a constant companion.

This cautionary tale highlights the dangers of poor money management, unraveling a journey from comfort to chaos—and the lessons we can draw from it.

The Allure of Financial Freedom

Imagine a young professional named Rahul, full of dreams and ambition. He recently landed his first job and is excited about the possibilities ahead. With his newfound independence, Rahul starts spending on things he had always wanted—designer clothes, the latest gadgets, fancy dinners, and frequent weekend trips. After all, he deserves to enjoy life after years of hard work, right?

What Rahul doesn't realize is that his paycheck, although generous, isn't limitless. Like many people, he assumes his future income will always cover his present spending.

But life is unpredictable. One small change—a surprise medical expense, an unexpected car repair, or even a company layoff—could turn his world upside down.

The Rise of Financial Stress

As time goes on, Rahul begins to notice his savings account doesn't grow despite his salary increases. Credit card bills start piling up, and he's paying more in interest than on the actual purchases.

The initial excitement of owning luxury items fades when repayment deadlines loom.

Then, the unexpected happens—his company undergoes restructuring, and his job is no longer secure. Rahul's once carefree life becomes riddled with anxiety. He struggles to meet monthly obligations, let alone save for the future.

This is where financial stress takes root, affecting not only his bank account but his mental health, relationships, and overall well-being.

Common Pitfalls of Poor Money Management

Rahul's story, unfortunately, mirrors the experiences of many individuals. It isn't about bad luck—it's about avoidable mistakes.

Here are some of the key pitfalls that lead to financial stress:

Living Beyond Means
Spending more than you earn may provide short-term happiness but creates long-term financial instability. Buying on credit without considering repayment terms traps people in debt cycles.

Ignoring Budgeting
A budget isn't a punishment—it's a plan for financial freedom. Without tracking expenses, it's easy to overspend on non-essentials while neglecting priorities like savings and investments.

Over-Reliance on Debt
Credit cards and loans might feel like an easy solution, but they often come with high interest rates. Carrying a balance month after month creates unnecessary financial pressure.

Lack of Emergency Savings
Life is unpredictable. Without a safety net, even small emergencies can spiral into major crises.

Procrastinating Investments

Postponing investments, especially in one's 20s and 30s, means losing out on the benefits of compound interest. This delay can significantly impact long-term financial security.

The Ripple Effect of Financial Stress

Financial stress doesn't exist in isolation. It affects every aspect of life, often in ways people don't anticipate.

Here's how it manifests:

Health Consequences
Constant worry about money can lead to sleep disturbances, anxiety, and depression. Over time, chronic stress impacts physical health, increasing the risk of illnesses such as heart disease and hypertension.

Strained Relationships
Money is one of the leading causes of conflict in relationships. Financial difficulties often create tension between partners, friends, or family members, eroding trust and communication.

Lost Opportunities
Financial instability limits opportunities for growth. Whether it's turning down a dream job in another city or missing out on investment opportunities, poor money management keeps people stuck in survival mode.

Diminished Self-Worth
Being unable to meet financial obligations can lead to feelings of shame and inadequacy, making it harder to seek help or take corrective actions.

Breaking the Cycle: Key Lessons
Rahul's downward spiral isn't unique, but it doesn't have to be permanent. Poor money management can be corrected with awareness, discipline, and proactive steps.

Here are the lessons his story teaches us:

Track Every Dollar
Financial clarity begins with knowing where your money goes. Maintain a record of income and expenses to identify unnecessary spending.

Build an Emergency Fund
Start small if necessary, but aim to save at least three to six months' worth of living expenses. This buffer can turn crises into manageable inconveniences.

Prioritize Needs Over Wants
Differentiate between essentials (like rent and groceries) and luxuries (like that new phone upgrade). It's okay to treat yourself occasionally, but not at the expense of financial health.

Limit Credit Card Usage
Use credit cards responsibly by paying off balances in full each month. Avoid taking on debt for non-essential items.

Start Investing Early
The earlier you start, the more time your money has to grow. Even small, consistent contributions to retirement accounts or mutual funds can lead to significant returns over time.

Seek Professional Advice
If managing finances feels overwhelming, consult a financial planner. An expert can help create a personalized plan tailored to your goals and situation.

Adopt a Growth Mindset
Mistakes are inevitable, but they're also learning opportunities. Instead of dwelling on past missteps, focus on building a better future.

A Happier Ending

Rahul eventually recognized the need for change. With the help of a friend who was financially savvy, he began taking small but significant steps toward better money management. He created a budget, reduced his reliance on credit cards, and committed to saving a portion of his income every month.

The transformation didn't happen overnight, but it did happen. Over time, Rahul rebuilt his financial stability and regained control of his life.

The lessons he learned made him more resilient, prepared, and confident in handling money.

Poor money management is a silent enemy, creeping into lives unnoticed until financial stress becomes overwhelming. But it doesn't have to end in despair.

By understanding common pitfalls and taking proactive steps, anyone can break free from the cycle of financial stress and build a future of security and abundance.

Rahul's cautionary tale serves as a reminder that financial health is as important as physical and emotional well-being. With the right tools and mindset, anyone can turn their story into one of success, proving that it's never too late to make a change.

Empowering Confidence Through Smart Money Management

Money management is not just about balancing numbers in a ledger; it is about creating a life of freedom, stability, and confidence.

For many, money represents a source of stress, but when managed effectively, it becomes a tool for unlocking dreams and securing peace of mind.

The True Meaning of Financial Freedom

Financial freedom isn't about becoming a millionaire overnight or living in endless luxury. It is about having control over your money, rather than letting it control you. Imagine waking up every morning knowing that you have enough to cover your needs, work toward your dreams, and handle unexpected challenges.

That sense of security is what financial freedom offers—a life where money is no longer a source of constant anxiety.

When you manage your money well, you free yourself from the cycle of paycheck-to-paycheck living. This freedom doesn't mean you stop working; instead, it means you work with purpose and passion, not out of fear or desperation.

Financial freedom is the ability to make choices—choices about your career, your lifestyle, and your future—without being shackled by financial stress.

The Confidence Boost from Money Management

Managing your money well brings an incredible boost to your self-confidence. Each time you pay off a debt, save a little more, or stick to your budget, you reinforce the belief that you are in control of your life.

This sense of control spills over into other areas, making you feel more empowered to tackle challenges and seize opportunities.

For instance, let's say you've been diligently saving for months, and an unexpected opportunity to invest in a passion project arises. Because you've managed your money well, you're not just financially ready—you're emotionally ready to take that leap.

The knowledge that you've prepared for such moments gives you confidence in your ability to make sound decisions.

Breaking the Chains of Stress

Money stress is one of the most common sources of anxiety worldwide. Whether it's worrying about bills, unexpected emergencies, or retirement, financial concerns can weigh heavily on your mind.

Poor money management exacerbates this stress, leading to sleepless nights and strained relationships.

When you take charge of your finances, however, you break free from this cycle. Budgeting, saving, and planning aren't just financial tools; they're stress management tools.

A well-structured financial plan serves as a safety net, catching you when life throws the unexpected your way.

For example, imagine your car breaks down, and the repair bill is steep. If you have an emergency fund in place, you won't panic. Instead, you'll calmly pay the bill and move on with your life, knowing you've prepared for moments like this. That calmness is priceless, and it comes from managing your money with intention and care.

Gaining Time and Energy

One of the most overlooked benefits of good money management is the time and energy it frees up. When your finances are in disarray, you spend countless hours worrying, planning, or scrambling to make ends meet. This mental and emotional drain leaves little room for creativity, relaxation, or personal growth.

On the other hand, effective money management streamlines your life. With a budget in place and your savings growing, you spend less time worrying about where your next dollar will come from. This newfound mental space can be devoted to your passions, hobbies, or simply spending quality time with loved ones.

Building a Legacy

Good money management doesn't just benefit you; it benefits future generations. Whether it's providing for your children's education, leaving a legacy for your family, or contributing to causes you care about, managing your money well allows you to make a lasting impact.

When you're financially stable, you can also serve as a role model for those around you. Imagine teaching your children or younger relatives the value of budgeting and saving, equipping them with skills that will serve them for a lifetime. The ripple effect of your good financial habits can inspire others to seek their own path to financial freedom and confidence.

Practical Steps to Financial Freedom

Achieving financial freedom and confidence doesn't happen overnight, but it's entirely possible with consistent effort and the right strategies.

Here are some actionable steps to get you started:

Create a Realistic Budget
A budget is the foundation of financial freedom. Start by listing your income and expenses, and ensure that you're living within your means. Allocate a portion of your income to savings and investments, even if it's a small amount at first.

Build an Emergency Fund
Life is full of surprises, and an emergency fund acts as your financial cushion. Aim to save three to six months' worth of living expenses in a separate account for unexpected situations.

Pay Off Debt Strategically
High-interest debt, like credit card balances, can be a significant obstacle to financial freedom. Focus on paying off these debts as quickly as possible, using strategies like the snowball or avalanche method.

Invest in Your Future
Saving for retirement, investing in stocks, or contributing to a pension plan are all ways to secure your financial future. The earlier you start, the more time your money has to grow.

Educate Yourself
Financial literacy is key to managing your money well. Read books, take courses, or consult with financial advisors to deepen your understanding of personal finance.

Set Clear Goals
Having specific financial goals gives you direction and motivation. Whether it's buying a home, starting a business, or traveling the world, clear goals help you stay focused and disciplined.

Reaping the Rewards
The rewards of managing your money well extend far beyond numbers on a spreadsheet. It's the freedom to take a vacation without guilt, the confidence to pursue a career change, and the peace of mind knowing your family is secure.

It's the ability to dream big and take risks, knowing you have a solid financial foundation to fall back on.

Most importantly, good money management allows you to live life on your own terms. It transforms money from a source of stress into a source of empowerment, enabling you to build a life filled with purpose, joy, and possibility.

Managing money well is a journey, not a destination. There will be challenges and setbacks along the way, but each step you take brings you closer to the freedom and confidence you deserve. Remember, financial freedom isn't about how much you earn; it's about how well you manage what you have.

With patience, discipline, and a clear plan, you can turn money into a powerful ally on your path to a better life.

Budgeting Templates and Tools for Financial Success

Budgeting might sound like a dry topic, but it's the secret sauce that transforms financial chaos into clarity. Whether you're living paycheck-to-paycheck or striving to save for your dreams, having a clear budgeting system is crucial. We'll dive into practical budgeting templates, explore the popular 50/30/20 rule, and introduce you to a treasure trove of apps and tools designed to make expense tracking and saving effortless.

Understanding Budgeting Templates

Budgeting templates are like maps that help you navigate your financial landscape. They provide structure, keep your spending in check, and help you prioritize your goals. The good news? You don't need to be a math whiz to use them!

Spending Tracker Template

A spending tracker is your starting point. It's a simple way to understand where your money is going. By recording every dollar you spend, you'll uncover spending habits that you didn't even realize you had.

Key Components:

Date: Record when the expense happened.
Category: Group your expenses (e.g., groceries, rent, entertainment).
Amount: Note the exact amount spent.
Need vs. Want: Was this purchase essential or discretionary?
Example:

Date	Category	Amount	Need/Want
Nov 25	Groceries	$50	Need
Nov 26	Coffee	$4.50	Want
Nov 27	Internet Bill	$60	Need

At the end of the month, review your tracker to spot patterns. Are you eating out too often? Spending too much on impulse buys? These insights are the first step toward smarter financial decisions.

50/30/20 Budgeting Template

The 50/30/20 rule is a simple yet effective guideline for managing your income.

Here's how it works:

50% for Needs: Allocate half of your income to essentials like rent, groceries, utilities, and insurance.
30% for Wants: Use this portion for non-essentials, such as dining out, streaming subscriptions, or hobbies.
20% for Savings and Debt Repayment: Reserve the rest for building savings, investing, or paying down debts.

How to Create a 50/30/20 Template:

Category	Monthly Budget (Based on $3,000 Income)	Actual Spending	Variance
Needs	$1,500	$1,400	+$100
Wants	$900	$1,000	-$100
Savings	$600	$600	$0

This template lets you compare your budgeted amounts to actual spending, making adjustments as needed.

Why Templates Work

Templates simplify decision-making and reduce the mental load of budgeting. Instead of wondering how much to save or spend, the structure does the work for you.

Plus, it makes financial discussions (with a partner or family) more transparent and organized.

The Best Apps and Tools for Expense Tracking and Saving

Technology has revolutionized how we handle money. Gone are the days of manually balancing checkbooks or poring over receipts. Today, apps and tools can automate, categorize, and even analyze your spending habits.

Expense Tracking Apps

Mint
Tracks spending, sets budgets, and provides a financial snapshot.
Automatically links to your bank accounts and credit cards.
Free to use, with robust insights into spending patterns.

YNAB (You Need A Budget)
Encourages proactive budgeting by assigning every dollar a job.
Helps users plan for upcoming expenses and avoid overspending.
Paid subscription, but it's a favorite for serious budgeters.

PocketGuard
Tells you exactly how much "pocket money" you have after covering essentials.
Great for beginners who want a quick, clear overview.
Features spending limits to help you stay on track.

Goodbudget
Based on the envelope budgeting method.
Helps you divide your money into virtual "envelopes" for each category.
Ideal for those who prefer a manual yet visual approach.

Spendee
Offers vibrant visuals to track income and expenses.
Supports family or group budgeting, perfect for shared expenses.
Available in free and premium versions.

Saving Apps

Acorns
Rounds up your purchases to the nearest dollar and invests the spare change.
Great for hands-off saving and investing beginners.

Qapital
Lets you create saving rules (e.g., "Save $5 every time I skip coffee").
Encourages saving through gamification and creativity.

Digit
Analyzes your spending habits and saves small amounts automatically.
Designed for those who struggle to save intentionally.

Honeydue
A budgeting app for couples, making it easier to track joint finances.
Encourages communication and transparency around money.

Simple (Banking App)
Combines banking with budgeting tools.
Features "Goals" to help you save for specific purposes.

Tools for Managing Debts and Investments

Debt Payoff Planner
Helps you strategize debt repayment by comparing methods like avalanche or snowball.
Visualizes progress with charts and timelines.

Personal Capital
Ideal for tracking both budgeting and investments.
Offers tools for retirement planning and net worth calculations.
Creating Your Personalized Budgeting System

Using templates and apps isn't a one-size-fits-all process.

Here's how to tailor them to your needs:

Assess Your Financial Situation
Start by gathering data: income, recurring expenses, debts, and savings. Use a spending tracker for at least one month to understand your habits.

Choose a Budgeting Method
If simplicity is your goal, the 50/30/20 rule is an excellent starting point. For more granular control, explore envelope budgeting or zero-based budgeting with apps like YNAB.

Set Clear Goals
Are you saving for a vacation, paying off student loans, or building an emergency fund? Having specific goals keeps you motivated.

Automate Where Possible
Use apps to automate savings or bill payments. The less you have to think about it, the more consistent you'll be.

Review and Adjust
Budgeting isn't a "set it and forget it" process. Life changes, so your budget should, too. Review it monthly to ensure it aligns with your priorities.

Budgeting doesn't have to feel restrictive—it's a tool for freedom. When you control your money, you can focus on what truly matters: achieving your dreams and living with less stress.

Whether you prefer templates, apps, or a combination of both, the key is to start. Take small, consistent steps, and over time, you'll transform your financial future.

Chapter 5: Earning the Rich Dad Way

In life, the difference between financial success and struggle often lies not in how hard you work, but in how you think about money and wealth. The Rich Dad way of earning is about developing a mindset that values creativity, strategic thinking, and resourcefulness. It's not about working harder but working smarter. Let's explore the principles that guide this transformative approach.

1. Mindset Shift: From Employee to Entrepreneur

The Rich Dad way begins with a significant mindset shift. Many of us are conditioned to think like employees—seeking job security, fixed salaries, and climbing the corporate ladder. However, Rich Dad teaches us to adopt an entrepreneurial mindset. This means looking for opportunities where others see obstacles, focusing on creating value rather than merely exchanging time for money, and embracing calculated risks.

An employee earns based on hours worked, but a Rich Dad seeks to create systems that generate income even while he sleeps. This could be through investments, businesses, or intellectual property. The idea is to move from the "time-for-money" trap into the realm of passive or semi-passive income streams.

2. Building Assets, Not Just Income

A core principle of earning the Rich Dad way is understanding the difference between assets and liabilities. An asset is something that puts money in your pocket, while a liability takes money out. For instance, a rental property that generates positive cash flow is an asset. In contrast, a fancy car that depreciates and costs you in maintenance is a liability.

Rich Dad focuses on acquiring and building assets.

This might include:

Real estate investments: Properties that generate rental income. Stocks and bonds: Investments that grow in value or pay dividends.

Businesses: Companies or side hustles that generate profits.

Intellectual property: Books, patents, or online courses that provide royalties or ongoing income.

The secret is reinvesting income from these assets to acquire even more assets, creating a cycle of wealth growth.

3. The Power of Financial Literacy

Most people struggle financially because they lack basic financial knowledge. The Rich Dad way emphasizes continuous learning about money—how it works, how to manage it, and how to make it grow.

This involves:

Understanding how taxes work and finding ways to legally minimize them. Learning how to read financial statements to evaluate the health of businesses or investments. Gaining knowledge about inflation, interest rates, and economic cycles.

The better your financial literacy, the more equipped you are to make informed decisions that maximize your earning potential.

4. Leveraging Other People's Resources

Rich Dad doesn't try to do everything alone. Instead, he leverages the power of other people's money (OPM), time, and expertise.

For instance:

Other People's Money: By taking loans or attracting investors, Rich Dad can fund business ideas or real estate projects without using his savings.

The returns generated often far outweigh the cost of borrowing.

Other People's Time: By hiring skilled professionals or building a team, Rich Dad focuses on strategic decision-making while delegating operational tasks.

Other People's Expertise: Collaboration with experts allows Rich Dad to access specialized knowledge and insights that improve the chances of success.

This principle isn't about exploitation but about creating win-win scenarios where everyone benefits.

5. Multiple Streams of Income

Relying on a single source of income is risky. The Rich Dad way involves diversifying income streams.

Think of your income sources as pillars holding up your financial house. If one pillar weakens, the others provide support.

Examples of diverse income streams include:

A primary business or job.
Rental income from properties.
Dividends from stocks.
Online businesses or digital products.
Royalties from creative works.

By diversifying, Rich Dad reduces financial vulnerability and increases opportunities for wealth growth.

6. The Value of Networking

Rich Dad understands the power of relationships in earning and building wealth. Surrounding yourself with like-minded, ambitious individuals opens doors to opportunities you might never have found alone. Networking provides access to potential partnerships, mentorship, and even clients or investors.

The saying, "Your network is your net worth," holds true. Successful networking is about building genuine, mutually beneficial relationships, not just collecting contacts.

7. Adopting a Long-Term Perspective

Many people focus on short-term gains, but Rich Dad thinks long-term.

For instance:

He invests in assets that may take years to yield significant returns but provide consistent growth over time.

He resists the temptation of instant gratification, choosing instead to reinvest profits to compound wealth.

He builds businesses with a vision for sustainability, not just short-lived profits.

Patience and discipline are crucial. By staying focused on long-term goals, Rich Dad ensures enduring success.

8. Embracing Technology and Innovation

Rich Dad recognizes that technology is a game-changer in earning potential. From e-commerce platforms to digital marketing, technology has opened new avenues for income.

By staying updated on trends and innovations, Rich Dad can capitalize on emerging opportunities.

For instance:

Creating an online course once and earning from it repeatedly is a modern example of leveraging technology.

Investing in tech startups or cryptocurrencies involves understanding new markets and taking calculated risks.

Automating businesses using software tools reduces operational costs and increases efficiency.

9. Learning from Failures

The road to wealth is rarely smooth. Rich Dad sees failures not as defeats but as stepping stones to success.

Every setback offers a lesson, and every challenge is an opportunity to grow. This resilience is key to earning and sustaining wealth.

For example, if a business venture fails, Rich Dad analyzes what went wrong, adapts his strategy, and applies the lessons to future endeavors.

This mindset ensures that mistakes become valuable learning experiences.

10. Giving Back to Multiply Wealth

Interestingly, the Rich Dad way isn't just about accumulating money for personal gain. Giving back—whether through charity, mentoring others, or contributing to the community—is a crucial part of the philosophy.

By creating value for others, Rich Dad not only helps society but often discovers new opportunities and networks that further enhance his earning potential. This principle also fosters a sense of purpose, making the journey of wealth creation more fulfilling.

The Takeaway

The Rich Dad way of earning isn't a get-rich-quick scheme. It's a thoughtful, disciplined approach to building sustainable wealth by changing your mindset, focusing on assets, leveraging resources, and continuously learning. It's about playing the long game, understanding that wealth isn't just about money—it's about freedom, security, and the ability to live life on your own terms.

By adopting these principles, anyone can begin the journey from struggling financially to achieving true financial independence. The key is to take action, stay committed, and always think like a Rich Daddy.

Unconventional Paths to Wealth

The journey to financial independence is often depicted as a rigid path: study hard, secure a high-paying job, and save diligently for decades. However, this traditional narrative doesn't suit everyone. In a rapidly changing world, unconventional methods of building wealth have emerged, offering opportunities to anyone willing to think outside the box. These paths—through side hustles, passion projects, and skill monetization—demonstrate that creativity, persistence, and adaptability can lead to financial success. Let's explore some inspiring stories of individuals who defied convention and discovered their unique roads to wealth.

The College Dropout Who Made Millions Teaching Online

When Sarah dropped out of college due to financial struggles, she thought her dreams of a stable career were over. She had always excelled at graphic design, teaching herself through free YouTube tutorials and practice.

Unsure how to monetize her skills, Sarah began by freelancing on platforms like Fiverr and Upwork.

Her big break came when she uploaded a few design tutorials on YouTube to help others. These videos attracted a modest audience, but more importantly, they led to requests for in-depth courses.

Recognizing an opportunity, Sarah launched her first online course on a popular e-learning platform. With clear instructions and engaging content, her course quickly gained traction, earning her thousands of dollars within months.

Fast-forward a few years, and Sarah now earns a six-figure income annually from online courses, consultations, and partnerships. What started as a side hustle became a life-changing passion project, allowing her to share her expertise while achieving financial independence.

The Hobbyist Who Turned a Love for Baking into a Business

Mark had always loved baking. His weekends were spent experimenting with recipes in his tiny kitchen, gifting cakes and pastries to friends and family. For years, he thought of it as nothing more than a fun pastime. That changed when a friend suggested he sell his treats at a local farmer's market.

With no formal training or business experience, Mark started small, baking from home and setting up a simple stall. The response was overwhelming—his unique flavors and homemade touch stood out in a sea of commercial options.

Encouraged by the feedback, Mark created an Instagram page to showcase his work and take orders online.

Within a year, Mark's side hustle grew into a full-fledged bakery, complete with a loyal customer base and collaborations with local cafes. His story is a testament to the power of passion. By turning a beloved hobby into a business, Mark found both personal fulfillment and financial success.

The Artist Who Leveraged Social Media for Global Reach

Maria, a self-taught painter from a small town, always dreamed of making a living through her art. But in a saturated market, she struggled to sell her work.

Determined to reach a wider audience, Maria turned to social media, posting videos of her creative process and sharing stories behind her pieces.

Her authenticity resonated with viewers, and her follower count skyrocketed. Maria soon began receiving commissions from across the globe. Additionally, she monetized her content through ad revenue, collaborations, and selling digital prints.

Maria's journey highlights how social media can democratize opportunities. With minimal upfront investment, she built a global art business, proving that even niche talents can flourish in today's connected world.

The Gamer Who Built a Career Playing Video Games

Jason's parents often scolded him for spending too much time playing video games, calling it a "waste of time." Little did they know it would become his career. Jason started streaming his gameplay on Twitch, initially as a hobby. His charismatic personality and exceptional skills drew viewers, and he began earning through donations, subscriptions, and sponsorships.

Beyond streaming, Jason diversified his income by creating YouTube content, selling merchandise, and participating in gaming tournaments. Today, he earns more in a month than he once did in a year at his 9-to-5 job.

His story shows that even unconventional interests, like gaming, can lead to financial success when combined with dedication and innovation.

The Teacher Who Found Wealth in Writing

Emily was a high school teacher who loved crafting stories but never thought writing could pay the bills.

Encouraged, Emily wrote more books, improving her craft and marketing skills along the way. Over time, her earnings from book royalties surpassed her teaching salary.

Writing, which started as a side hustle, became her primary source of income and a way to connect with readers worldwide.

The Fitness Enthusiast Who Built a Brand

Liam was a fitness enthusiast with no formal background in business. He worked as a personal trainer but found it hard to scale his income due to time constraints.

To reach more clients, Liam began sharing workout tips and challenges on social media.

His approachable style attracted thousands of followers, leading to brand partnerships and the launch of his own line of fitness products. Liam also created an affordable online fitness program, allowing him to help people globally while generating passive income.

His journey underscores the potential of combining expertise with digital tools to achieve financial growth.

The Family Who Found Freedom Through Real Estate

The Thompsons were an average middle-class family, living paycheck to paycheck. They decided to try real estate investing, starting with a small duplex they could afford.

Living in one unit and renting out the other, they discovered the power of passive income.

Over the years, they reinvested their earnings into more properties, gradually building a portfolio that provided financial stability and freedom.

While the path required sacrifices and a steep learning curve, the Thompsons' success exemplifies how ordinary families can build wealth through strategic decisions.

Lessons Learned

The stories above share common themes:

Start Small: Most of these journeys began with minimal resources or risk. Whether it was teaching online, selling baked goods, or leveraging social media, small steps laid the foundation for long-term success.

Leverage Technology: Digital platforms have made it easier than ever to monetize skills, connect with audiences, and scale businesses. From e-learning to social media, these tools offer endless opportunities.

Embrace Unconventional Ideas: Many of these individuals succeeded by pursuing paths others overlooked.

Their willingness to explore nontraditional avenues set them apart.

Adapt and Learn: Continuous learning and adaptability were key.

Whether it was improving their craft or mastering marketing, these individuals invested in their growth.

Persistence Pays Off: None of these success stories happened overnight. Each required time, effort, and resilience in the face of setbacks.

Your Path Awaits

The beauty of unconventional wealth-building is that it's accessible to everyone. Whether you're a passionate hobbyist, a skilled professional, or someone with a dream, there's a path for you.

Start small, embrace creativity, and persist in your efforts. Your journey may not follow the conventional roadmap, but it can lead to extraordinary destinations.

Make Poor Dad Rich Dad is not just about building wealth—it's about building a life that aligns with your passions, values, and aspirations. Let these stories inspire you to take the first step toward your financial transformation.

Diversify Your Income Streams: Starting Right Where You Are

The idea of diversifying income streams may sound complex, like something only seasoned entrepreneurs or wealthy investors can achieve.

However, the truth is that anyone, no matter where they are in life, can begin to diversify their income streams. It starts with small steps, creativity, and a clear understanding of your resources and abilities.

Why Diversify Your Income?

Relying solely on one source of income, such as a single job, leaves you vulnerable. Unexpected events like layoffs, economic downturns, or personal emergencies can disrupt that income stream. Diversifying your income is like building a safety net; it gives you financial security and freedom to pursue what truly matters in life.

It also creates opportunities to grow wealth over time, allowing you to live on your terms rather than being tied to a paycheck.

Assess Your Current Position

Before diving into creating multiple income streams, take stock of your current situation.

Ask yourself:

What skills do I already have?
Consider both your professional expertise and hobbies. Are you a great writer, graphic designer, or cook? Do you enjoy teaching, crafting, or fixing things?

How much time can I commit?
If you work full-time, you might only have evenings and weekends. Be realistic about how much energy and time you can dedicate without overwhelming yourself.

What resources are available to me?
Resources include your network, savings, or even items you own. Maybe you have a car, a camera, or access to a space that could help generate income.

What are my financial goals?
Define your goals. Are you trying to pay off debt, save for a vacation, or build long-term wealth? Your goals will guide your efforts.

Step 1: Start with What You Know

Begin by monetizing skills or hobbies you already possess. This is the easiest and most efficient way to start because it doesn't require additional training or certifications.

Freelancing: Websites like Fiverr, Upwork, or LinkedIn can connect you with clients who need your expertise, whether it's writing, graphic design, coding, or even voice-over work.

Tutoring: If you excel in a particular subject, offer tutoring services. This can be academic (like math or science) or non-academic (such as music or cooking).

Selling handmade goods: Platforms like Etsy or local craft fairs are great for selling handmade products like jewelry, art, or home decor.

Example:

Mary, a full-time teacher, started tutoring students in her spare time. She found a demand for SAT prep and eventually created an online course, turning her teaching skills into a profitable side hustle.

Step 2: Leverage Your Existing Assets

You may have underutilized resources that can generate income. Rent out space: If you have a spare room or an unused garage, list it on platforms like Airbnb or use it for storage rentals through websites like Neighbor.

Use your vehicle: Sign up for ridesharing services like Uber or Lyft, or deliver food and packages through apps like DoorDash or Instacart.

Sell unused items: Declutter your home and sell items on eBay, Facebook Marketplace, or Poshmark.

Example:

John, who owned a large backyard, started hosting small outdoor events. Over time, he transformed his space into a cozy venue, earning extra income every weekend.

Step 3: Invest Wisely for Passive Income
Passive income is money earned with minimal ongoing effort. While it often requires upfront investment, even small amounts can make a difference over time.

Stock market: Start small with apps like Robinhood or Acorns, which allow you to invest spare change. Look into index funds or ETFs for long-term, low-risk growth.

Real estate crowdfunding: Platforms like Fundrise allow you to invest in real estate projects with as little as $500.

Dividend-paying stocks: Certain companies pay dividends to shareholders, providing regular income just for owning their stock.

Example:

Lisa, a nurse, started investing $50 a month in index funds. Ten years later, her portfolio had grown significantly, supplementing her regular income.

Step 4: Create Digital Products

The digital world offers limitless opportunities to generate income from content creation.

E-books and online courses: Write an e-book on a topic you know well or create an online course using platforms like Teachable or Skillshare.

Blogging or YouTube: Share your expertise or hobbies through blogs or videos. Monetization comes through ads, sponsorships, and affiliate marketing.

Stock photography or templates: If you're good at photography or design, sell your work on platforms like Shutterstock, Canva, or Creative Market.

Example:

Jake, a fitness enthusiast, created workout plans and sold them online. Eventually, he built a following on social media, leading to sponsorship deals and merchandise sales.

Step 5: Explore the Gig Economy

Short-term, flexible jobs can provide extra income without a long-term commitment.

Pet sitting or dog walking: Apps like Rover make it easy to connect with pet owners in need of services.

Event staffing: Sign up with local staffing agencies to work part-time at events.

Mystery shopping: Get paid to evaluate customer service at stores and restaurants.

Example:

Sophie, a college student, earned extra money by babysitting and mystery shopping on weekends, helping her graduate debt-free.

Step 6: Partner with Others

Sometimes, collaboration is the key to creating a new income stream.

Start a business with a friend: Combine your skills with someone else's to create a venture, like a catering service, photography business, or tutoring center.

Invest in others: If you have savings, consider micro-lending or funding a small business in your community.

Affiliate marketing: Partner with companies to promote their products and earn commissions.

Example:

Tom and Sarah teamed up to start a weekend food truck. Tom handled cooking while Sarah managed marketing.

The venture became so successful that it eventually replaced their full-time jobs.

Step 7: Automate and Scale

Once you've established a few income streams, look for ways to automate and scale them. This could mean outsourcing tasks, using software to manage processes, or reinvesting profits to grow the business.

Use tools: Automate tasks like invoicing, email marketing, or social media posts.

Delegate: Hire freelancers or part-time workers to handle tasks that take up too much of your time.

Expand your audience: Focus on growing your reach, whether through social media, advertising, or collaborations.

Example:

Emma started a blog that earned modest ad revenue. By hiring a virtual assistant to handle content scheduling, she had more time to focus on creating high-quality posts, doubling her traffic and income.

Challenges and How to Overcome Them

Diversifying your income isn't always smooth sailing. You may face obstacles like time constraints, lack of resources, or fear of failure.

Here's how to tackle them:

Start small: You don't need to make huge investments or sacrifices. Begin with something manageable and grow from there.

Educate yourself: Learn through free resources like YouTube, podcasts, or community workshops.

Stay consistent: Progress may be slow at first, but persistence is key.

The Power of a Diverse Portfolio

By diversifying your income streams, you not only protect yourself from financial instability but also open the door to opportunities you might not have imagined. Each stream, no matter how small, contributes to your financial independence and peace of mind.

Remember, the goal isn't to overwhelm yourself by trying to do everything at once. Start with one or two ideas that resonate with you and build from there. Over time, these small efforts will snowball into a more secure and fulfilling financial future.

Your journey to diversifying income streams starts today—with what you already have, where you are. Take that first step, and watch your efforts grow into something remarkable

Unleashing the Side Hustle Potential in You

Starting a side hustle can transform your financial future, unlock hidden talents, and help you build wealth. Whether you're looking to break free from paycheck-to-paycheck living or simply add a new revenue stream, the key is taking action. In this section of Make Poor Dad Rich Dad, we'll focus on two essential steps: brainstorming a side hustle and crafting a 30-day action plan to get started.

Worksheet: Brainstorming Side Hustle Ideas Based on Your Skills and Passions

Side hustles are most successful when they align with what you're good at and what excites you.

To uncover those opportunities, follow this guided brainstorming worksheet:

1. Identify Your Skills

Take a moment to list the skills you've gained through your education, career, or hobbies. Think broadly—skills don't have to be technical.

Here are some categories to consider:

Professional Skills: Writing, graphic design, coding, teaching, public speaking, marketing.

Creative Skills: Photography, crafting, painting, cooking, sewing.
Technical Skills: IT troubleshooting, video editing, spreadsheet expertise.

Soft Skills: Communication, leadership, problem-solving, empathy.

Worksheet Prompt:
Write down at least 5-10 skills you have:

2. Explore Your Passions
Now, think about the things you love doing, regardless of whether they're directly related to your skills. Passion fuels perseverance, which is critical for any side hustle.

Reflect on these questions:
What activities make me lose track of time?
What problems in the world would I love to solve?
What hobbies do I genuinely enjoy?

Worksheet Prompt:

List 5-10 things you are passionate about:
1. ....
2. ....
3. ....
4. ....
5. ....

3. Spot the Overlap

Combining skills and passions is the sweet spot for sustainable side hustles.
Use the following matrix to discover intersections:

Skill	Passion	Potential Side Hustle
Teaching	Baking	Start a baking workshop for beginners
Photography	Traveling	Offer travel photography services
Writing	Environmental Advocacy	Create a blog or eBook on eco-living

Fill out this chart with your unique combinations. Write down 3-5 ideas that resonate with you.

4. Validate Your Ideas

Not every idea will work out, so narrow your list using these criteria:

Market Demand: Is there an audience for this service or product?
Profitability: Can it bring in enough income to meet your goals?
Time Commitment: Is it feasible alongside your current responsibilities?

Worksheet Prompt:

Circle or highlight your top 2-3 ideas that check all the boxes.

5. Define Your Why

Having a strong reason to pursue a side hustle keeps you motivated. Write down your "why" in one sentence:
"I want to start this side hustle because _____."

Action Plan: Start a Side Hustle in 30 Days

Once you've chosen a side hustle, it's time to take action.

Here's a step-by-step, 30-day plan to help you launch confidently:

Week 1: Research and Preparation
Define Your Offer:
Write a clear description of your side hustle idea. What problem does it solve? Who is it for?

Example:

Side Hustle: Resume writing services.
Target Audience: Job seekers transitioning careers.
Problem Solved: Creating impactful resumes that stand out.

Market Research:
Study competitors. What do they offer? How do they price their services?
Survey potential customers to validate demand.

Set Goals:
Define a financial target (e.g., "Earn $500 in my first month").
Break it into weekly objectives.

List Tools and Resources:

Write down everything you need to get started:
Website or social media account?
Tools like Canva, Etsy, or Fiverr?
Week 2: Create and Test Your Product/Service

Build a Prototype or Portfolio:

If you're selling a product, create a sample or mockup.
For services, gather testimonials or showcase past work in a portfolio.

Test Your Idea:

Offer your product/service to a small audience (e.g., friends or family) for feedback.

Ask questions like:
"What do you like about this?"
"What can be improved?"

Adjust Based on Feedback:
Refine your offer based on what you learn.
Week 3: Marketing and Visibility

Create a Basic Online Presence:

Launch a social media profile (e.g., Instagram, LinkedIn).
Build a simple website or landing page using tools like Wix or WordPress.

Content Strategy:

Post engaging content about your side hustle (e.g., tips, behind-the-scenes, customer stories).
Use visuals and clear calls-to-action to encourage people to reach out.

Networking:

Share your side hustle with your personal network.
Join online communities or local groups where your target audience hangs out.

Announce Your Launch:

Share your side hustle widely on social media, email, and word-of-mouth.

Use an irresistible offer for your first customers (e.g., discounts, freebies).

Track Results:

Monitor key metrics: income, website visits, social media engagement.

Optimize:

Tweak your pricing, messaging, or services based on performance.

Plan for Growth:

Set up recurring systems to save time (e.g., scheduling tools, automated emails).
Brainstorm how you can expand (e.g., upselling, partnerships).

Building Wealth, One Hustle at a Time

Starting a side hustle doesn't have to be overwhelming. By following the structured worksheet and 30-day action plan above, you'll move from brainstorming to launching with clarity and confidence. Remember, your side hustle isn't just about extra income; it's about creating opportunities for growth, freedom, and wealth.

Chapter 6: The Power of Financial Networking

Imagine you're standing in a room full of people. Some are chatting in small groups, others are exchanging business cards, and a few are discussing investment opportunities.

Now imagine that each of these people has access to knowledge, resources, and opportunities that could potentially transform your financial future.

This room is your network—a network that can become your most powerful tool for achieving wealth and financial success. Welcome to the concept of financial networking.

Financial networking is the art and science of building and maintaining relationships with people who can contribute to your financial growth.

It is not about asking for money or favors but about creating genuine connections that lead to mutual benefit. This concept might sound straightforward, but its potential is extraordinary.

A well-cultivated network can open doors to opportunities you didn't even know existed, guide you through complex financial decisions, and provide the support and inspiration needed to achieve your goals.

Why Financial Networking Matters

Wealth is rarely built in isolation. Even the most successful entrepreneurs and investors will tell you that their achievements are a product of not only their own efforts but also the support and input of their networks.

Here's why financial networking is so impactful:

Access to Opportunities

Opportunities are everywhere, but they are often hidden behind doors that only a strong network can unlock. Whether it's a new job, a promising investment, or a partnership, networking puts you in touch with people who can introduce you to these opportunities. For example, a conversation with an acquaintance might lead to discovering an emerging industry ripe for investment or an insider tip about a business venture looking for partners.

Shared Knowledge and Insights

No one knows everything about money, investments, or wealth creation. Networking allows you to tap into the collective knowledge of others. Experienced mentors, financial advisors, and peers in your network can offer valuable insights into markets, trends, and strategies. They can help you avoid costly mistakes and provide guidance tailored to your unique situation.

Support System

Financial journeys can be daunting, filled with risks and uncertainties. A strong network acts as a support system, offering encouragement and advice during challenging times. People in your network can also help you navigate failures, which are often inevitable on the path to success.

Increased Visibility

Networking enhances your visibility in financial and professional circles. As more people become aware of your skills, goals, and ambitions, you are more likely to attract opportunities that align with your aspirations. Visibility is especially crucial for entrepreneurs, as it can lead to potential investors, collaborators, and clients.

How to Build a Financial Network

Building a financial network is not a one-time event; it is an ongoing process that requires effort, authenticity, and a strategic approach.

Here are practical steps to get started:

Start with the People You Know
Your initial network begins with family, friends, and colleagues. These are people who already trust you and are likely to support your growth. Talk to them about your financial goals and ask for introductions to others who might share your interests.

Expand Strategically
Attend events, workshops, and seminars related to finance, investing, or entrepreneurship. Joining professional associations and online communities can also connect you with like-minded individuals.

Choose events and groups that align with your financial goals to ensure you're meeting the right people.

Be Authentic and Generous
Networking isn't about taking; it's about giving and building relationships. Be genuinely interested in others, listen to their stories, and look for ways to help them.

Offering value, whether it's sharing your expertise or connecting someone to a resource, builds trust and goodwill.

Leverage Social Media
Platforms like LinkedIn, Twitter, and specialized forums are invaluable for connecting with professionals and thought leaders.

Share insightful content, engage with others' posts, and participate in discussions to build your online presence and credibility.

Maintain and Nurture Relationships

Building a network is just the beginning; maintaining it is equally important. Keep in touch with people regularly, even if it's just a quick message or a comment on their post. Celebrate their successes and show genuine interest in their lives.

The Role of Mentors and Advisors

Mentors and financial advisors are key players in your financial network. A mentor is someone who has walked the path you aspire to follow. They can provide invaluable guidance, share lessons from their experiences, and help you avoid pitfalls. Finding the right mentor involves identifying someone you admire and reaching out with humility and genuine curiosity.

Financial advisors, on the other hand, are professionals who can offer expert advice tailored to your goals. They can help with budgeting, investment planning, and wealth management. While hiring an advisor often involves a fee, their insights can save you significant time and money in the long run.

The Ripple Effect of Networking

One of the most powerful aspects of networking is its ripple effect. When you help someone in your network, they are more likely to help you in return. Moreover, your act of generosity might inspire others to do the same, creating a chain reaction of support and opportunities.

This ripple effect amplifies the impact of your network and reinforces the idea that financial success is a collaborative effort.

For instance, imagine you connect a friend to a job opportunity. That friend might later introduce you to an investor who becomes a crucial part of your business journey. Each connection builds on the last, creating a web of relationships that strengthen over time.

The Challenges of Financial Networking

While financial networking is a powerful tool, it comes with its challenges. Building trust takes time, and not every connection will lead to immediate results. Rejection is also a possibility—some people might not respond to your outreach or show interest in connecting. The key is persistence and understanding that networking is a long-term investment.

Another challenge is maintaining authenticity. In the pursuit of opportunities, it's easy to fall into the trap of focusing solely on what you can gain. Remember that true networking is about creating win-win relationships. Approach every interaction with the mindset of giving, and the benefits will naturally follow.

Financial networking is not just a skill; it's a mindset and a lifestyle. By building and nurturing a network of like-minded individuals, mentors, and advisors, you can unlock opportunities, gain valuable insights, and receive support on your journey to financial success.

The power of financial networking lies in its ability to amplify your potential through relationships. It's about understanding that wealth is not just measured in money but in the connections and collaborations that make achieving your goals possible. So, step into the room, start building those connections, and watch as your network transforms into one of your greatest financial assets.

The Power of Connection

In the small coastal town of Bellehaven, where everyone knew each other's names, lived a man named Arjun. He wasn't wealthy, nor did he come from a family of privilege. In fact, his family had lived in a modest house for generations, running a struggling grocery store that barely made ends meet.

However, Arjun had something invaluable: an unshakable belief in the power of relationships.

From a young age, Arjun had been fascinated by the way people interacted.

While others focused on their studies or business strategies, Arjun spent his time engaging with customers, neighbors, and even strangers who visited Bellehaven. "People are the real currency," his late mother had once told him, and those words stayed with him like a guiding light.

A Serendipitous Encounter

One sunny afternoon, Arjun was restocking shelves in the store when a tourist walked in. The man, dressed casually but carrying an air of confidence, looked lost. Arjun struck up a conversation.

"Looking for something specific?" he asked with his usual warm smile.

The man chuckled. "Actually, I'm just exploring the town. It's my first time here."

"Welcome to Bellehaven!" Arjun replied enthusiastically. "You should check out the lighthouse—it has the best views. Oh, and if you're hungry, don't miss Mira's café down the street."

The two ended up talking for nearly an hour. Arjun learned that the man, Ravi, was an entrepreneur visiting small towns to scout for potential business opportunities.

Ravi, in turn, was struck by Arjun's genuine interest in people and his natural ability to connect.

Before leaving, Ravi handed Arjun his business card. "If you're ever in the city, look me up," he said. "I think you'd be great at something I'm working on."

The Leap of Faith

Months passed, and life in Bellehaven continued as usual. But Arjun couldn't shake the memory of his conversation with Ravi. Though he had no concrete plan, he decided to reach out. Gathering his courage, he sent Ravi an email, reminding him of their chat and expressing interest in learning more about his work.

To Arjun's surprise, Ravi responded almost immediately. He invited Arjun to the city to attend a networking event he was hosting. Arjun hesitated. He had never left Bellehaven for something so uncertain, and the trip would cost more than he was comfortable spending.

But deep down, he knew this could be the opportunity of a lifetime.

With his father's reluctant blessing, Arjun boarded a bus to the city. Clutching Ravi's business card and wearing his only formal shirt, he arrived at the event—a dazzling gathering of entrepreneurs, investors, and innovators.

The Ripple Effect of Networking

At first, Arjun felt out of place. The room buzzed with conversations about technology, investments, and growth strategies—worlds far removed from his life in Bellehaven. But he reminded himself of his strength: connecting with people.

He started introducing himself, sharing his story and asking questions about others' work. One conversation led to another, and soon Arjun found himself talking to a woman named Priya, who was launching a project to bring sustainable farming techniques to rural areas. Priya was intrigued by Arjun's deep understanding of his hometown's challenges and invited him to join her team as a local advisor.

But the surprises didn't stop there. Another attendee, impressed by Arjun's humility and insights, offered to mentor him in business strategy. Through these connections, Arjun began to see a future beyond the grocery store—a future where he could make a real difference not just for his family but for his entire community.

Turning Opportunities into Impact

With Priya's project, Arjun returned to Bellehaven, introducing sustainable farming practices that transformed the town's struggling agriculture. Farmers who had been on the brink of giving up found new hope and prosperity.

Meanwhile, under his mentor's guidance, Arjun revamped the family grocery store, turning it into a hub for locally sourced, organic produce. The store became a model for small businesses in the region, attracting media attention and even government support.

The most unexpected turn came a year later when Ravi invited Arjun to co-found a social enterprise focused on empowering rural entrepreneurs.

Drawing on his experiences in Bellehaven, Arjun played a key role in designing programs that helped small-town businesses thrive.

Lessons Learned

Looking back, Arjun often marveled at how one conversation had changed his life. It wasn't luck, he realized—it was the result of being open, curious, and willing to take a chance.

"Networking isn't about collecting contacts," he often told aspiring entrepreneurs. "It's about building genuine relationships. You never know who might see potential in you or where a simple conversation could lead."

For Arjun, networking had turned a life of limitations into one filled with possibilities. He proved that you don't need wealth or a prestigious background to achieve greatness; you just need the courage to connect and the determination to act on the opportunities that come your way.

The Bigger Picture

Today, Arjun's story is a testament to the transformative power of networking. Through his connections, he didn't just uplift his family but also brought lasting change to his community. His journey shows that every interaction holds the potential for growth, and even the smallest town can be the starting point for something extraordinary.

The lesson is clear: never underestimate the power of a simple hello, a thoughtful question, or an open mind.

In the world of networking, every door you open could lead to opportunities you never imagined.

The Power of Connections: Fast-Tracking Your Success

Success is rarely a solo journey. The truth is, the people you surround yourself with play a significant role in how quickly you achieve your goals. Think of connections as bridges; some lead directly to where you want to go, while others might offer valuable detours or surprising shortcuts. Building and nurturing the right relationships is one of the most effective ways to fast-track your success.

Imagine you're climbing a mountain. You could choose the hardest path, navigating steep cliffs and loose rocks on your own. Or, you could meet someone who knows the terrain well, someone who can point out the safest route or offer a rope to help you scale faster. Connections work the same way in life and business. The right people can help you avoid mistakes, provide access to resources, and open doors that might have otherwise remained closed.

Shared Knowledge and Expertise

When you connect with people who have experience in your field, you gain access to a treasure trove of insights. These individuals have likely faced challenges similar to yours and can guide you through potential pitfalls. A single conversation with the right person can save you months, even years, of trial and error.

Opportunities You Can't See Alone

Sometimes, the biggest opportunities aren't advertised. They're hidden within networks. Someone you know might recommend you for a job, partnership, or project you didn't even know existed. This phenomenon, often called the "hidden job market," is a testament to the power of being connected.

Boosted Credibility

The company you keep matters. Being associated with well-respected individuals or groups can enhance your reputation. When people see that someone credible trusts or supports you, they're more likely to give you opportunities or take you seriously.

Motivation and Support

Surrounding yourself with ambitious, driven people creates an environment where success is contagious. These connections can provide encouragement, hold you accountable, and push you to aim higher.

It's important to remember that building connections is not about using people for personal gain. It's about creating genuine, mutually beneficial relationships.

People are more willing to help when they see you as someone who adds value to their lives too.

Stepping Out of Your Comfort Zone

The Key to Building Meaningful Relationships

Building strong connections requires effort and courage, especially if you're naturally shy or reserved.

However, the best things often come when you step out of your comfort zone.

Let's explore how you can do this effectively:

1. Start Small, but Start Somewhere

It's easy to feel intimidated when thinking about building relationships, especially if you're picturing large networking events or making cold introductions to influential people. Instead, begin with smaller steps. Strike up conversations with colleagues, neighbors, or even acquaintances at a local coffee shop.

These low-pressure interactions can help you build confidence and prepare you for more significant opportunities.

2. Attend Events and Gatherings

Whether it's a conference, workshop, or even a casual meetup in your community, putting yourself in environments where like-minded people gather is essential. At first, it might feel uncomfortable, but remember, everyone there is human and probably feels the same nerves as you.

When you attend these events, have a few conversation starters prepared. Ask open-ended questions like, "What brought you here today?" or "What's been the most exciting part of your work recently?"

These questions show interest in the other person, making them more likely to engage with you.

3. Volunteer or Collaborate

Volunteering is a fantastic way to meet people while contributing to a cause you care about. It's also an organic way to build relationships, as you'll be working alongside others with shared values.

Similarly, collaborating on projects—whether at work or in personal endeavors—provides opportunities to connect deeply with others.

4. Embrace Rejection as a Learning Opportunity

Not every connection attempt will result in a meaningful relationship, and that's okay. Rejections or awkward moments are part of the process. Instead of taking them personally, view them as learning experiences.

Over time, you'll develop better instincts for approaching and engaging with people.

5. Learn to Listen Actively

One of the most powerful ways to build relationships is to genuinely listen. Many people focus on what they'll say next instead of being present in the conversation.

By truly listening and responding thoughtfully, you demonstrate respect and empathy—qualities that make others more likely to connect with you.

6. Expand Your Comfort Zone Gradually

Building relationships doesn't mean you have to become a social butterfly overnight. Expand your comfort zone in manageable increments. For instance, if you're uncomfortable speaking in groups, practice speaking one-on-one first. Once that feels natural, challenge yourself to engage in group settings.

7. Follow Up and Stay Connected

Meeting someone once is only the beginning. The real relationship develops when you make an effort to stay in touch. Send a follow-up message, share an article you think they'd find interesting, or invite them for coffee.

Regular, authentic communication is key to maintaining connections over time.

The Transformative Power of Relationships

When you step out of your comfort zone to build relationships, you're not just gaining connections—you're transforming yourself. Each interaction helps you grow more confident, empathetic, and resourceful.

Over time, what once felt daunting becomes second nature, and you'll find yourself effortlessly forming bonds that enrich both your personal and professional life.

The right connections can act as a multiplier for your efforts, accelerating your progress toward your dreams. But it's up to you to take that first step: to introduce yourself, to reach out, and to show genuine interest in others.

Success isn't just about what you know; it's also about who you know—and how you treat them.

As you navigate your journey, remember that every interaction is an opportunity.

With intentionality, effort, and a willingness to step outside your comfort zone, you can build a network that not only supports your success but inspires others to achieve their objectives.

Templates for Networking Messages and Social Media Profiles

Networking is one of the most valuable skills for personal and professional growth.

Knowing how to create meaningful connections can open doors to opportunities, mentorships, collaborations, and even new career paths.

But to make the most out of networking, it's important to know how to communicate effectively, both in written and verbal form.

This section provides practical templates for networking messages and crafting a strong LinkedIn and other social media profiles to maximize your networking potential.

Templates for Networking Messages

Networking messages can serve different purposes, from introducing yourself to following up on a conversation or requesting advice.

Below are some templates tailored for different scenarios:

1. Reaching Out for the First Time (Cold Outreach):

This is when you're connecting with someone you don't know personally. Your message should be concise and respectful of their time.

Template:

Hi [Name],

I came across your profile while researching [industry/topic], and I was impressed by your work in [specific achievement/project]. I'm currently [your role/field of interest], and I'm eager to learn more about [specific topic].

If you have a few minutes, I would greatly appreciate any advice you could share or insights into your journey in [industry]. Thank you for your time, and I hope to connect with you soon!

Best regards,
[Your Name]

2. Following Up After a Meeting or Event:

When you've already met someone at an event or networking session, follow up to keep the connection alive.

Template:

Hi [Name],

It was great meeting you at [event name]. I really enjoyed our conversation about [specific topic]. I've been reflecting on [something specific they mentioned], and it has given me valuable perspective on [your relevant work/interest].

I'd love to stay connected and perhaps explore [a shared interest or topic]. Thank you again for your time, and I look forward to staying in touch!

Best regards,
[Your Name]

3. Asking for a Referral or Introduction:

If you're seeking a referral or want someone to introduce you to a connection of theirs, be clear and polite.

Template:

Hi [Name],

I hope this message finds you well! I'm currently exploring opportunities in [industry/field] and noticed that you're connected with [person's name]. I admire their work in [specific area], and I believe speaking with them could provide valuable insights for my journey.

If you're comfortable, would you be willing to introduce me to [person's name]? I'd deeply appreciate the opportunity to connect and learn more. Thank you in advance for your help!

Best regards,
[Your Name]

4. Requesting a Coffee Chat or Informational Interview:

When seeking advice or insight, offer a simple request without pressuring the recipient.

Template:

Hi [Name],

I've been following your work in [industry/topic], and I find it incredibly inspiring. I'm currently [describe your role/goals], and I'm eager to learn more about your experience in [specific area].

If your schedule permits, I'd love to buy you a coffee (or have a quick virtual chat) to hear more about your career journey and any advice you might have for someone starting in this field. I understand you're busy, so even a brief conversation would mean a lot.

Thank you for considering my request, and I hope we can connect soon!

Warm regards,
[Your Name]

5. Maintaining and Nurturing Connections:

Staying in touch with your network over time is just as important as making new connections.

Template:

Hi [Name],

I hope you're doing well! I wanted to reach out and say hello. I've been [briefly share an update about yourself], and it reminded me of our previous conversation about [topic].

I'd love to hear how you're doing and if there's anything exciting happening in your world. Let me know if you'd like to catch up sometime soon!

Best regards,
[Your Name]

Crafting an Effective LinkedIn and other Social Media Profiles

Your LinkedIn and other social media profiles are your digital business cards. It's often the first impression potential employers, collaborators, or mentors will have of you.

Here's how to optimize each section of your profile:

1. Profile Photo:
Choose a high-quality, professional-looking photo where you appear approachable. Dress in a way that reflects your industry.

2. Headline:
Your headline is more than your job title—it's your personal brand. Highlight your expertise or goals.

Example:
"Data Analyst | Turning Numbers into Strategic Insights | Passionate About Sustainable Solutions"

3. About Section:
The "About" section is your elevator pitch. Write a concise and engaging summary of who you are, your professional background, and what drives you.

Example:
"As a digital marketing specialist with over 5 years of experience, I thrive on crafting data-driven strategies that drive engagement and growth. I'm passionate about storytelling, analytics, and creating impactful campaigns that resonate with audiences. When I'm not optimizing campaigns, I enjoy mentoring aspiring marketers and exploring the latest tech trends."

4. Experience:
Use bullet points to highlight your achievements rather than just listing responsibilities. Quantify your impact wherever possible.

Example:

Increased website traffic by 40% through targeted SEO strategies.
Spearheaded a social media campaign that resulted in a 20% rise in customer engagement.

5. Skills and Endorsements:

List your key skills, and ask connections to endorse you for them. This builds credibility.

6. Recommendations:
Request recommendations from colleagues, mentors, or clients. These testimonials add weight to your profile.

7. Activity Section:
Engage with posts, share your thoughts, or write articles on topics you're passionate about. This establishes you as an active contributor in your field.

A "Network Map" Exercise to Evaluate and Expand Connections Building a strong network requires understanding who you already know and identifying where to expand. The network map exercise helps you visualize your connections and uncover opportunities for growth.

Steps to Create a Network Map

1. Start with a Core Circle:
Write down the names of your closest connections—people you interact with frequently, like family, friends, colleagues, and mentors.

2. Identify Categories of Connections:

Group your connections into categories such as:

Personal: Friends, family, and acquaintances.
Professional: Colleagues, supervisors, and industry peers.
Academic: Professors, classmates, and alumni.
Aspirational: People you admire but haven't connected with yet.

3. Visualize Your Network:

Create a simple diagram with yourself in the center and these groups branching out. Use sub-branches to list individuals under each category.

4. Evaluate Your Network:

Ask yourself:
Are there gaps in certain areas?
Are you relying too heavily on one group?
Are you connected to people in your target industry or role?

5. Expand Strategically:
Based on your evaluation, set goals for expanding your network.

For example:
Attend industry events or webinars to meet professionals in your field.
Reconnect with old contacts through a friendly message.
Leverage LinkedIn to find and connect with people in roles you aspire to.

6. Track Progress:
Periodically revisit your network map to add new connections and review your growth.

Making Connections Count

Networking is not just about meeting people—it's about building genuine relationships. Invest time in understanding others' goals and finding ways to support them.

With thoughtful communication, a polished LinkedIn and other social media presence, and an intentional approach to growing your network, you can unlock endless opportunities.

Chapter 7: Investing Like Rich Dad

Investing is one of the most crucial habits that differentiate the financially struggling from the financially successful. To invest like Rich Dad, one must embrace a mindset of growth, focus on opportunities, and build a disciplined approach to wealth creation.

Unlike Poor Dad, who might shy away from investments due to fear of loss or lack of knowledge, Rich Dad uses investments as a powerful tool to grow wealth and secure financial freedom.

The Philosophy Behind Investing Like Rich Dad

Rich Dad views money as a tool, not a goal. Instead of working solely for money, Rich Dad makes money work for him.

This philosophy stems from the belief that wealth is not just about earning; it's about multiplying what you earn. Every dollar Rich Dad earns is treated like a potential employee, whose job is to bring in more dollars.

For Poor Dad, the idea of investing can feel risky or overwhelming. Poor Dad often focuses on saving, assuming it's the safest path. While saving is essential, inflation gradually erodes the value of money sitting idle.

Rich Dad knows this and emphasizes the importance of making money grow faster than inflation through smart investments.

Key Principles to Invest Like Rich Dad

1. Start Early, No Matter How Small

Rich Dad knows the power of compound interest, which Albert Einstein famously called the "eighth wonder of the world." The earlier you start investing, the more time your money has to grow. Even small amounts invested consistently can grow into significant wealth over time.

For example, investing $100 per month in a mutual fund with a 10% annual return can grow to over $200,000 in 30 years.

If you're late to the game, don't worry. The best time to start was yesterday; the second best is today. Focus on starting now and catching up through disciplined, consistent contributions.

2. Diversify Your Investments

Rich Dad believes in not putting all eggs in one basket. Diversification reduces risk by spreading investments across various asset classes like stocks, bonds, real estate, mutual funds, and even alternative investments such as gold or cryptocurrencies.

Poor Dad might invest all his money in one "safe" option, such as a savings account or a single property. Rich Dad, on the other hand, knows that markets fluctuate and a balanced portfolio ensures stability.

By diversifying, losses in one area can often be offset by gains in another.

3. Invest in Assets, Not Liabilities

One of Rich Dad's golden rules is understanding the difference between assets and liabilities. An asset puts money into your pocket, while a liability takes money out.

For example, a rental property generating monthly income is an asset, but a car with ongoing expenses and depreciation is a liability. Before investing, ask yourself: Will this generate income or appreciate in value? If not, reconsider.

Rich Dad prioritizes building a portfolio of assets that consistently generate cash flow, such as dividend-paying stocks, rental properties, or businesses.

4. Educate Yourself Continuously

Investing is not gambling. Rich Dad makes informed decisions by staying updated on market trends, learning about new financial instruments, and seeking expert advice. He reads books, listens to podcasts, and attends seminars to sharpen his knowledge.

Poor Dad might avoid investing due to a lack of understanding, but Rich Dad believes that knowledge minimizes risk. Take the time to learn basic financial literacy concepts such as risk, return, inflation, and compounding. This foundation will help you make better decisions.

5. Embrace Calculated Risks

Every investment involves some level of risk, but Rich Dad doesn't shy away from it. Instead, he manages risk through research, diversification, and preparation.

For instance, Rich Dad doesn't jump into the stock market blindly. He studies companies, analyzes financial reports, and understands market trends before investing. He is not afraid of failure, knowing that setbacks are often stepping stones to success.

Poor Dad, on the other hand, might avoid all risk, missing out on opportunities to grow wealth. Rich Dad advises balancing your portfolio to align with your risk tolerance while aiming for long-term gains.

6. Focus on Long-Term Growth

Rich Dad invests with patience, recognizing that wealth-building is a marathon, not a sprint. He avoids chasing quick profits or following market fads, instead focusing on investments with steady, long-term potential.

For example, instead of selling stocks during a market dip out of fear, Rich Dad holds onto them, understanding that markets historically recover and grow over time. This patience pays off as he benefits from compound growth.

7. Leverage Passive Income Streams

Rich Dad prioritizes creating income streams that don't require active daily effort. Passive income allows your investments to work for you even while you sleep.

This might include investing in rental properties, dividend stocks, or peer-to-peer lending platforms. Poor Dad often relies solely on earned income, exchanging time for money. Rich Dad, however, seeks to reduce dependence on active income by building a strong portfolio of passive income-generating assets.

8. Utilize Tax-Advantaged Accounts

Rich Dad is strategic about taxes. He understands that maximizing post-tax returns is as important as choosing the right investments. Tax-advantaged accounts, such as 401(k)s, IRAs, or other retirement savings plans, allow money to grow tax-free or tax-deferred, significantly boosting returns over time.

Poor Dad often overlooks these benefits, missing out on valuable tax savings. Rich Dad advises using these accounts to your advantage, especially if your employer offers matching contributions.

Steps to Begin Your Investment Journey

Assess Your Financial Situation

Start by analyzing your current finances. Determine how much money you can allocate toward investments without jeopardizing your daily needs or emergency savings.

Set Clear Goals
Define your investment objectives, whether it's buying a home, funding education, or retiring early. Clear goals help guide your investment strategy.

Choose the Right Investment Platforms
Research platforms that match your investment style. For instance, beginners might prefer robo-advisors, while experienced investors may choose brokerage accounts for direct trading.

Start Small but Stay Consistent
Don't wait for the perfect moment or a large sum of money. Begin with what you have and invest consistently. Automating your investments can help you stay disciplined.

Monitor and Rebalance Your Portfolio
Periodically review your investments to ensure they align with your goals. If one asset class grows disproportionately, rebalance your portfolio to maintain diversification.

Learning from Mistakes
Even Rich Dad has made mistakes, but he treats them as valuable lessons.

Poor Dad might dwell on failures and avoid future opportunities, but Rich Dad analyzes what went wrong and improves his strategy.

Remember, no investor has a perfect track record. Success comes from learning and adapting.

A Legacy of Wealth

Rich Dad doesn't just invest for himself; he invests to create a legacy. By building wealth through smart investments, he ensures financial security for future generations. Poor Dad often struggles to pass down wealth because he prioritizes short-term needs over long-term growth.

Rich Dad's approach demonstrates that investing isn't just about money—it's about freedom, security, and the ability to live life on your terms. By adopting these principles, you too can transition from a mindset of scarcity to one of abundance.

Take your first step today, and let your investments pave the way to a brighter financial future.

First-Time Investor's Journey to Financial Growth

The Journey Starts with Awareness

Financial independence is a goal shared by many, yet achieving it often feels daunting, especially for first-time investors. The idea of transitioning from a "poor daddy" mindset—living paycheck to paycheck, burdened by debt—to a "rich daddy" mindset—strategically growing wealth through disciplined habits—requires knowledge, planning, and a shift in perspective.

Understanding the Starting Point:

A Case Study of Sarah's Financial Awakening

Sarah, a 28-year-old teacher, lived in a rented apartment in Chicago, relying entirely on her monthly salary of $3,200. While passionate about her profession, Sarah often felt anxious about her finances. She had student loan debt of $25,000, credit card debt of $5,000, and no significant savings. The thought of investing was overwhelming—she assumed it was reserved for wealthy individuals with disposable income.

Sarah's turning point came during a casual conversation with her friend Josh, who mentioned his modest success in investing. Intrigued, Sarah asked questions and realized that investing wasn't a distant dream but a practical step toward financial security.

Encouraged by Josh's advice, she resolved to begin her journey toward financial growth.

Step 1: Education and Mindset Shift

Before diving into investments, Sarah spent three months educating herself. She enrolled in free online courses about personal finance, read books about financial independence, and consumed podcasts on money management.

The key lessons she learned included:

Pay Yourself First: Sarah started setting aside 10% of her income ($320 monthly) for savings and investments.

Understand Compound Interest: She grasped the power of compounding, realizing how small, consistent investments grow significantly over time.

Set Clear Goals: Sarah wrote down her financial objectives, such as paying off her debts within three years, building an emergency fund, and growing a retirement portfolio.

Armed with these insights, Sarah shifted from a scarcity mindset to an abundance mindset. She stopped seeing money as something she lacked and started viewing it as a tool for growth.

Step 2: Creating a Financial Plan

Sarah's next step was to create a realistic financial plan tailored to her circumstances. She listed her expenses and identified areas where she could cut costs.

For example, she replaced her $200/month gym membership with free YouTube workout routines and meal-prepped to reduce her dining-out expenses. These changes freed up an additional $400 per month, which she funneled toward her financial goals.

Sarah divided her surplus income as follows:

Debt Repayment: $300/month toward her credit card debt.
Emergency Fund: $200/month until she accumulated three months' worth of expenses.
Investments: $220/month to begin her portfolio.

Step 3: Taking the First Investment Steps

Once Sarah saved $1,000 in her emergency fund, she opened an account with a beginner-friendly investment platform. With guidance from her research and a financial advisor she consulted, Sarah decided to:

Start Small with Index Funds: She chose a low-cost S&P 500 index fund to diversify her portfolio without needing expert knowledge. This decision aligned with her long-term goal of steady growth.

Leverage a Retirement Account: Sarah contributed $150 monthly to a Roth IRA, taking advantage of tax benefits while planning for the future.

Experiment with Fractional Shares: Curious about individual stocks, Sarah invested $70 in fractional shares of companies she understood and believed in, such as a tech firm and a consumer goods company.

Step 4: Staying Disciplined Amid Challenges

In her first year of investing, Sarah faced challenges, including market fluctuations and unexpected expenses. For instance, during a market dip, her portfolio's value decreased by 10%. Initially, she panicked and considered withdrawing her money. However, she recalled her lessons about long-term investing and resisted the urge.

Instead of succumbing to fear, Sarah continued her contributions, taking advantage of the lower prices during the dip (a strategy known as dollar-cost averaging). This decision proved beneficial when the market rebounded.

Step 5: Celebrating Small Wins and Adjusting the Plan

By the end of two years, Sarah had achieved significant milestones:
Debt-Free Status: She paid off her credit card debt and reduced her student loans to $15,000.
Emergency Fund: She saved $6,000, providing her with peace of mind during unforeseen events.
Investment Portfolio Growth: Her consistent investments grew to $7,200, with a 12% average annual return.

Encouraged by these results, Sarah increased her monthly contributions to $300. She also explored additional opportunities, such as contributing to her workplace 403(b) retirement plan to benefit from employer matching.

Lessons from Sarah's Journey

Sarah's story highlights several key lessons for first-time investors:

Start Where You Are: Even small amounts can lead to substantial growth when invested consistently.
Educate Yourself: Financial literacy empowers better decision-making and reduces fear of the unknown.

Stay Patient: The market fluctuates, but long-term investments reward patience and discipline.
Diversify Your Portfolio: Spreading investments across different asset classes minimizes risk and maximizes growth potential.
Celebrate Progress: Acknowledging small wins motivates continued efforts.

A Path Open to Everyone

Sarah's journey from financial anxiety to steady growth demonstrates that investing isn't reserved for the wealthy—it's a pathway accessible to anyone willing to learn, plan, and act.

By embracing a "Rich dad" mindset, focusing on education, and staying disciplined, first-time investors can build wealth and secure a brighter financial future.

Your story could be next. Start today, and take the first step toward transforming your financial reality.

Remember: wealth isn't just about money; it's about the freedom and opportunities that come with financial stability.

Breaking Down the Fear of Investing: Discovering Long-Term Benefits

For many people, the word "investing" brings up feelings of anxiety, uncertainty, and even fear. It's easy to understand why—financial jargon, unpredictable markets, and stories of losses can make investing seem like a gamble.

However, investing doesn't have to be scary. When approached with the right mindset and tools, it's one of the most powerful ways to grow your wealth over time.

Let's take a closer look at how to break down the fear of investing by focusing on its long-term benefits.

Why Are We Afraid to Invest?

Fear of investing often stems from three common misconceptions:

It's Too Risky.
Many believe that investing means putting money into something uncertain, where there's a high chance of losing it all. However, risk is not the same as loss. Risk can be managed, especially when investments are diversified and held for the long term.

It's Too Complicated.
Financial terms like "dividends," "mutual funds," and "asset allocation" might sound like a foreign language. This complexity can deter beginners. But the truth is, you don't need a finance degree to get started. Today, there are simple tools, guides, and even financial advisors to help you invest with confidence.

It's Only for the Wealthy.
Another myth is that investing is only for people who already have lots of money. In reality, investing is for everyone, no matter how small the starting amount. Even $10 a month can grow significantly over time.

The Power of Long-Term Thinking
One of the most effective ways to reduce the fear of investing is by understanding its long-term benefits. Think of investing as planting a tree. You nurture it, give it time, and eventually, it grows into something much larger than you started with.

As Albert Einstein famously said, "Compound interest is the eighth wonder of the world. He who understands it, earns it. He who doesn't, pays it." Compound interest means your money grows not only from the initial amount you invested but also from the returns it earns.

Over time, this growth can snowball, turning modest investments into significant wealth.

Let's break it down with an example:

Suppose you invest $200 per month starting at age 25 into an account that earns an average return of 7% annually. By the time you turn 65, your account could grow to nearly $500,000, even though you only contributed $96,000.

On the other hand, if you wait until age 35 to start, the total would be around $250,000—half as much—because you lost 10 years of compounding.

The takeaway? The earlier you start, the more time your money has to grow.
"Investing Is How Your Money Works While You Sleep"

A job pays you only while you're awake and working. But investments? They never sleep. They grow while you rest, take vacations, or spend time with family. That's the magic of having your money work for you.

Here's another way to look at it: imagine every dollar you invest as a tiny employee. The more you invest, the larger your "team" of employees becomes, working tirelessly to earn more for you.

Over the years, this team becomes stronger and more productive, helping you reach financial goals that once seemed out of reach.

The Historical Proof of Long-Term Benefits

History shows us that markets tend to grow over time despite short-term ups and downs. Take the U.S. stock market as an example.

Over the last century, the stock market has averaged around 7–10% annual returns, even with major downturns like the Great Depression, the 2008 financial crisis, and the COVID-19 pandemic.

If you invest wisely and stay committed for the long term, you can weather these storms and come out ahead.

The key is to avoid reacting emotionally to short-term fluctuations. Patience pays off.

Strategies to Overcome Fear

Start Small.
If you're nervous, begin with a small amount of money. Even a few dollars can help you learn the process and build confidence.

Educate Yourself.
Knowledge is a powerful antidote to fear. Read beginner-friendly books, listen to podcasts, or watch videos about investing.

The more you understand, the less intimidating it becomes.

Use Simple Tools.
Apps and robo-advisors like Acorns, Robinhood, or Wealthfront are designed to make investing easy. They guide you step-by-step and handle much of the complexity for you.

Set Clear Goals.
Knowing why you're investing makes it easier to stay focused. Are you saving for retirement, a home, or your child's education? Having a clear goal helps you stay committed even when the market fluctuates.

Think Long Term.
Always remind yourself that investing is a marathon, not a sprint. As Warren Buffett puts it, "Someone's sitting in the shade today because someone planted a tree a long time ago." Your investments today are creating shade for your future.

The Emotional Shift: From Fear to Confidence

As you take small steps and see progress, you'll notice your fear turning into confidence. The first time you see your investments grow, even by a tiny amount, you'll realize the power of compounding. Over time, you'll go from asking, "What if I lose money?" to thinking, "What else can I invest in?"

Beyond Wealth: The Freedom Factor

Investing isn't just about making money; it's about creating freedom. When your investments grow, you gain the ability to make choices. Whether it's retiring early, starting a business, or traveling the world, financial freedom opens doors to possibilities that fear would have kept locked.

Fear is natural, but it doesn't have to hold you back. By starting small, educating yourself, and focusing on long-term growth, you can turn investing into a tool that empowers you instead of intimidating you. Remember, "Investing is how your money works while you sleep." Every step you take today is a step toward a richer, freer future.

So, let's replace fear with action. Start planting your financial seeds today, and watch your wealth grow—one smart investment at a time.

A Beginner's Guide: How to Start Investing with $100
Why $100 is a Great Starting Point

Starting your investment journey doesn't require thousands of dollars. With $100, you can take meaningful steps toward financial independence.

The key is to start small, stay consistent, and understand that even small investments can grow significantly over time through the power of compounding. This guide will help you confidently take that first step.

Step 1: Set Clear Financial Goals

Before you invest, define your purpose. Are you saving for a specific goal, such as buying a car, funding education, or building wealth for retirement? Knowing why you're investing will help you decide where to put your money.

Goals also help you determine the time horizon—how long you're willing to wait to see returns—and the level of risk you're comfortable taking.

For example:

Short-term goal: Save for a vacation in a year.
Long-term goal: Build a retirement fund over 20 years.

Step 2: Understand the Basics

Investing involves putting money into assets that can grow in value over time. Common asset types include stocks, bonds, mutual funds, ETFs (exchange-traded funds), and alternative investments like real estate or cryptocurrencies. Each asset class has its unique risk and return characteristics, which you should match with your goals and risk tolerance.

Step 3: Choose Your Investment Platform

Today, investing $100 is easier than ever thanks to technology. Several apps and platforms let you start investing with a small amount.

Look for platforms that:

Have no account minimums or low fees.
Offer fractional shares (so you can buy parts of expensive stocks like Apple or Amazon).
Provide educational resources for beginners.
Popular platforms include Robinhood, Acorns, Stash, and Fidelity.

Step 4: Diversify Your Investment

One golden rule of investing is to diversify, or "not put all your eggs in one basket." With $100, you might think this is difficult, but modern tools make it possible through fractional investing and ETFs.

ETFs (Exchange-Traded Funds): ETFs allow you to invest in a collection of stocks or bonds, spreading your risk. For example, an S&P 500 ETF gives you exposure to 500 large U.S. companies for a single investment.

Fractional Shares: You can invest in small pieces of a company's stock, like buying $10 worth of Tesla instead of an entire share.

Step 5: Be Consistent and Patient

With $100, you might not see large gains immediately, but consistency is key. Regularly adding to your investments, even small amounts, can build substantial wealth over time. Consider setting up automatic contributions to your investment account.

Example: Starting a Portfolio with $100

Imagine you decide to invest $100 across different assets:
$50 in an S&P 500 ETF (for broad market exposure).
$30 in a bond ETF (for stability).
$20 in a single growth stock like a promising technology company.
This balanced portfolio spreads risk while offering growth potential.

Simple Examples of Investments with Varying Risk Levels

Understanding risk is essential to making informed investment decisions. Here are some examples of investments categorized by their risk levels: low-risk, medium-risk, and high-risk.

1. Low-Risk Investments

Low-risk investments provide safety for your principal (the amount you invest), but their returns are often lower. These are ideal for conservative investors or short-term goals.

Savings Accounts and CDs (Certificates of Deposit):

Example: Putting $100 in a high-yield savings account that earns 3% annually. After a year, your balance would grow to $103—safe but with limited growth.

CDs lock in your money for a specific period, offering slightly higher interest rates than savings accounts.

Government Bonds:

Example: Buying a U.S. Treasury bond for $100. These bonds are backed by the government, making them very secure. Over time, you receive your principal plus interest.

Money Market Funds:

Example: Investing $100 in a money market fund, which pools money into low-risk, short-term debt securities. Returns are slightly higher than savings accounts but still low-risk.

2. Medium-Risk Investments

Medium-risk investments balance growth and safety. They offer better returns than low-risk options but may experience moderate fluctuations.

Dividend-Paying Stocks:

Example: Buying $100 of a stock that pays regular dividends, such as Coca-Cola or Procter & Gamble. Dividends provide steady income, and the stock's value can grow over time.

Risk Level: Moderate—stock prices can fluctuate, but dividends cushion your investment.

Mutual Funds and ETFs:

Example: Investing in a balanced mutual fund with 60% stocks and 40% bonds. If the fund averages a 6% annual return, your $100 could grow to $106 in one year.

Risk Level: Moderate—varies depending on the fund's composition.

Real Estate Crowdfunding:

Example: Platforms like Fundrise allow you to invest $100 in real estate projects. Returns often come from rental income or property appreciation.

Risk Level: Moderate—real estate prices can rise or fall based on market conditions.

3. High-Risk Investments

High-risk investments have the potential for substantial gains but come with the possibility of losing part or all of your money. These are suitable for long-term goals or individuals comfortable with volatility.

Individual Growth Stocks:

Example: Investing $100 in a startup company's stock. If the company grows rapidly, your $100 could double or triple. However, if the business fails, your entire investment might be lost.

Risk Level: High—stock values can be unpredictable.

Cryptocurrencies:

Example: Buying $100 worth of Bitcoin. If Bitcoin's price rises, your $100 could grow significantly. However, cryptocurrencies are highly volatile and can lose value quickly.

Risk Level: Very High—prices can fluctuate by double-digit percentages in a single day.

Options Trading:

Example: Using $100 to buy call options for a stock you believe will rise. If your prediction is correct, your returns can be massive. If not, you lose your $100.

Risk Level: Very High—requires in-depth knowledge and is not recommended for beginners.

Tips for Managing Risk

Know Your Risk Tolerance: Understand how much risk you're willing to take. A simple way to assess this is to ask yourself how you would feel if your $100 dropped to $50 overnight.

Diversify Across Risk Levels: Spread your investments among low-, medium-, and high-risk options to balance potential losses and gains.

Invest for the Long Term: Markets fluctuate in the short term, but long-term investing tends to smooth out volatility.

Stay Informed: Keep learning about investment options, market trends, and economic conditions. An informed investor is a confident investor.

Starting with $100 might seem small, but it's the foundation of a larger financial journey.

By understanding risk levels and exploring diverse investment opportunities, you can make your money work for you, one step at a time.

Whether you prefer the stability of bonds, the balanced growth of ETFs, or the high potential of stocks, the key is to start now and stay consistent.

Chapter 8: Overcoming Setbacks and Failures

Life is rarely a straight path, and for many of us, setbacks and failures are inevitable. But what if we changed our perspective on them? Instead of seeing them as roadblocks, we could view them as steppingstones to success. In the journey to transform from a "Poor Dad" mindset to a "Rich Dad" mindset, learning to overcome setbacks is a critical skill.

Understanding Setbacks

A setback is not the end of the road—it's a bend in it. It could be a financial loss, a failed business venture, or even a missed opportunity. These challenges test our resilience and determination. The first step in overcoming setbacks is to recognize them for what they are: temporary obstacles, not permanent barriers.

Think of a setback as a lesson wrapped in disguise. Every financial loss or failure carries valuable insights. Perhaps a bad investment teaches you to conduct better research, or a failed side hustle highlights the importance of managing time effectively. Instead of dwelling on the disappointment, focus on extracting the lesson.

Embrace a Growth Mindset

The way we think about failure determines how we respond to it. A fixed mindset believes that abilities and intelligence are static, leading to avoidance of challenges for fear of failure.

A growth mindset, on the other hand, sees challenges as opportunities to grow and improve.

Adopting a growth mindset is crucial for financial success. Start by reframing your inner dialogue. Instead of saying, "I can't believe I messed up," say, "What can I learn from this experience?" By changing the narrative, you shift your focus from the problem to the solution.

Emotional Resilience: The Power of Bouncing Back

Failures often bring along an emotional toll—feelings of frustration, embarrassment, or self-doubt. Building emotional resilience helps you bounce back stronger.

Here are a few strategies:

Allow Yourself to Feel: It's okay to feel disappointed or upset. Acknowledge your emotions instead of suppressing them. This acknowledgment is the first step toward healing.

Talk It Out: Share your feelings with a trusted friend, mentor, or family member. Talking can provide new perspectives and alleviate the burden of carrying the setback alone.

Practice Gratitude: Even in difficult times, find something to be thankful for. Gratitude shifts your focus from what's wrong to what's still going well.

Analyzing Failures Objectively

Once the initial emotions have settled, it's time to analyze the setback objectively.

Ask yourself:
What went wrong?
Was this within my control?
What can I do differently next time?
Treat this analysis like a financial audit. Be honest and thorough without being overly critical of yourself. This process allows you to identify patterns or gaps in your decision-making and address them moving forward.

Building a Comeback Plan

Every comeback starts with a plan.

Here's a step-by-step approach to rebuild after a setback:

Define Your End Goal: Be clear about what you're aiming for. Whether it's regaining lost savings, rebuilding a business, or achieving a specific milestone, clarity is key.

Break It Down: Divide your goal into smaller, actionable steps. Each step should feel achievable, giving you a sense of progress as you move forward.

Seek Knowledge: Use the lessons learned from your failure to guide your next steps. Research, upskill, or consult experts to fill any knowledge gaps.

Take Action: Don't wait for the "perfect" moment—start now. Even small actions build momentum and reignite your confidence.

Stories of Resilience

History is filled with inspiring stories of individuals who overcame setbacks to achieve greatness. Thomas Edison famously said, "I have not failed. I've just found 10,000 ways that won't work." His relentless perseverance led to the invention of the light bulb.

In the financial world, many successful entrepreneurs experienced early failures. For example, Walt Disney faced bankruptcy and rejection before creating one of the most successful entertainment empires in history.

These stories remind us that failure is not the opposite of success; it's often a part of the journey to success.

The Role of Financial Safety Nets

One practical way to soften the impact of financial setbacks is to build a safety net. This can take the form of an emergency fund, diversified investments, or passive income streams. These safety nets provide stability, allowing you to recover without derailing your long-term goals.

Positive Habits to Prevent Future Setbacks

While you can't entirely avoid setbacks, cultivating certain habits can reduce their likelihood.

Continuous Learning: Stay informed about trends, market changes, and financial strategies. Knowledge is a powerful shield against poor decisions.

Risk Management: Evaluate risks carefully before making decisions. This includes financial risks, time investments, and potential opportunity costs.

Adaptability: Be willing to pivot when circumstances change. Flexibility often determines how well you handle unforeseen challenges.

Cultivating Self-Compassion

One of the hardest parts of overcoming failure is dealing with self-blame. Remember, you are human, and mistakes are part of the learning process.

Treat yourself with the same kindness and understanding you would offer a friend.

Self-compassion doesn't mean avoiding accountability—it means recognizing that setbacks are part of growth. By being gentle with yourself, you create a healthy foundation for improvement.

Celebrating Small Wins

As you work through setbacks, don't forget to celebrate progress along the way. Small wins, like sticking to a budget or saving a little extra each month, build momentum and confidence.

Celebrate these victories to remind yourself of how far you've come.

Staying Inspired

Finally, surround yourself with positivity. Read books, listen to podcasts, or join communities that motivate and uplift you. Inspiration fuels resilience and keeps you focused on your goals.

Turning Setbacks into Steppingstones

Overcoming setbacks is less about avoiding failure and more about learning to rise after falling. Each failure brings a chance to grow stronger, wiser, and more prepared for the future.

In your journey to transform into a "Rich Dad," embrace setbacks as part of the process. With the right mindset, tools, and support, you can turn every obstacle into an opportunity.

A Narrative of a Financial Failure and the Lessons Learned

In the world of personal finance, stories of failures often serve as the most profound teachers. One such story comes from the life of a man named Ravi, an entrepreneur who dreamed of launching a thriving café business in his hometown. Ravi was not wealthy but had always been passionate about coffee.

Inspired by popular café chains, he envisioned a warm, inviting space where people could unwind, work, or meet friends over a cup of expertly brewed coffee.

To kick-start his dream, Ravi pooled his savings, borrowed money from friends, and took a small bank loan. Brimming with enthusiasm, he rented a prime location and spared no expense in designing the perfect ambience. His café opened with a bang, attracting customers drawn to its cozy interiors and unique blends. For a few months, it seemed as though Ravi's dream was coming to life.

However, beneath the surface, trouble brewed. Ravi had overestimated the number of daily customers he would attract and underestimated his monthly expenses. Rent, utilities, employee wages, and inventory costs far exceeded his earnings.

He lacked a detailed business plan and hadn't accounted for seasonal variations in foot traffic. Furthermore, he did not track his cash flow closely, assuming initial losses were normal for any startup.

As debts mounted, Ravi began cutting corners to save costs. He reduced the quality of ingredients and let go of some staff, which hurt the café's reputation. Customers dwindled further, and within two years, Ravi had no choice but to shut down his beloved café. The financial failure left him heartbroken and in debt.

Lessons Learned

Ravi's story offers valuable lessons for anyone embarking on a financial or entrepreneurial journey.

Start Small and Scale Gradually: Ravi could have begun with a smaller, less expensive setup to test his idea before expanding. Starting small allows for learning without risking significant losses.

Plan Finances Carefully: A detailed financial plan, including cost estimations, revenue projections, and a buffer for unexpected expenses, could have saved Ravi from the crisis.

Monitor Cash Flow Closely: Ravi's failure to track income and expenses in real-time led to delayed recognition of the financial trouble. Regular financial reviews are critical for identifying and addressing issues early.

Adaptability Is Key: Instead of cutting corners, Ravi could have pivoted by offering services like coffee delivery or collaborating with local artists to host events, boosting visibility and income.

Don't Overleverage: Borrowing beyond one's capacity to repay can lead to catastrophic consequences. Ravi's heavy reliance on loans worsened his situation when the business didn't perform as expected.

Although Ravi lost his café, he did not lose his entrepreneurial spirit. Armed with the lessons from his failure, he started a small coffee subscription service that grew steadily over time. His journey highlights that failures, though painful, are stepping stones to success when viewed as opportunities to learn and improve.

Famous Examples of Resilience

The Case of Walt Disney and Others

Resilience is the cornerstone of financial and personal success. Few stories embody this truth more than that of Walt Disney, the creative genius who brought to life characters and stories beloved by generations.

Walt Disney: From Bankruptcies to a Legacy

Before Walt Disney became synonymous with success, he endured a series of crushing failures. In the early 1920s, Disney founded a small animation company in Kansas City called Laugh-O-Gram Studio. Despite his talent and passion, the company struggled to stay afloat due to poor financial management and a lack of paying clients. Eventually, Laugh-O-Gram Studio went bankrupt, leaving Disney penniless.

Rather than giving up, Disney moved to Los Angeles with little more than a suitcase and a few unfinished animation reels. There, he and his brother Roy founded the Disney Brothers Studio. Even then, success did not come easily.

His first major character, Oswald the Lucky Rabbit, was taken from him by a distributor, leaving Disney devastated.

Instead of succumbing to despair, Disney created a new character—Mickey Mouse—which became an instant sensation. This pivotal moment marked the beginning of his rise to fame and fortune. Over the years, Walt Disney faced additional challenges, including financial risks during the production of iconic films like Snow White and the Seven Dwarfs and the construction of Disneyland.

Yet his resilience and vision turned those risks into unparalleled successes. Today, the Walt Disney Company stands as a testament to his unwavering determination.

Oprah Winfrey: Rising Above Adversity

Another powerful example of resilience is Oprah Winfrey, who rose from poverty to become one of the world's most influential media moguls. Oprah's early life was marked by hardships, including financial struggles, abuse, and discrimination. She began her career as a news anchor but was fired from her first job because her bosses felt she was "unfit for television."

Instead of allowing rejection to define her, Oprah pursued opportunities that aligned with her strengths. Her ability to connect with audiences led to the launch of The Oprah Winfrey Show, which became a global phenomenon.

Through hard work, resilience, and a focus on authenticity, she built a media empire and became a billionaire. Oprah's story reminds us that setbacks are temporary and that perseverance can transform even the most difficult circumstances.

J.K. Rowling: From Welfare to Literary Stardom

The story of J.K. Rowling, the author of the Harry Potter series, is another powerful example of resilience. In the early 1990s, Rowling was a struggling single mother living on welfare.

Despite facing financial difficulties, she spent her free time writing the manuscript for Harry Potter and the Philosopher's Stone.

When she completed the book, Rowling faced a series of rejections from publishers who doubted its commercial viability. After 12 rejections, Bloomsbury Publishing finally agreed to publish the book, albeit with a small initial print run.

The rest, as they say, is history. Rowling's perseverance paid off, and the Harry Potter series became one of the best-selling book franchises in history, making her one of the richest women in the world.

Lessons from Resilient Leaders

Adaptability: Walt Disney's ability to create Mickey Mouse after losing Oswald exemplifies how adapting to challenges can lead to breakthrough ideas.

Faith in Vision: Oprah Winfrey's unwavering belief in her ability to connect with audiences drove her success despite initial failures.

Perseverance Against Rejection: J.K. Rowling's journey teaches us that persistence in the face of rejection is crucial to achieving one's goals.

Learning from Failure: All these individuals used their failures as opportunities to grow, improve, and refine their approach.

Failure and resilience are two sides of the same coin in the journey toward financial success. Whether through personal narratives like Ravi's or legendary examples like Walt Disney, Oprah Winfrey, and J.K. Rowling, the underlying message is clear: setbacks are not the end of the road but stepping stones to greater achievements.

By embracing failure as a learning experience and cultivating resilience, anyone can overcome obstacles and achieve their dreams. The key lies in maintaining focus, adapting to challenges, and believing in one's ability to rise again.

Failure is an inevitable part of life. Everyone, from the most celebrated entrepreneurs to everyday individuals, experiences setbacks.

Yet, the difference between those who succeed and those who give up lies in their mindset. Successful individuals view failure not as a final verdict but as a stepping stone toward growth and success.

The Nature of Failure

Failure often carries a negative connotation. It can evoke feelings of shame, disappointment, or even self-doubt. But what is failure, really? It's nothing more than an outcome that didn't align with our expectations.

It's important to remember that failure isn't a reflection of your worth but a temporary result of your actions.

Think of a child learning to walk. They stumble and fall countless times. Yet, they don't label themselves as failures. Instead, they instinctively use each fall to adjust their balance, strengthen their muscles, and try again.

This persistence eventually leads to success. So why should adults view failure any differently?

Failure as Feedback: A New Perspective

When you view failure as feedback, it transforms from an emotional burden into a valuable teacher.

Feedback is information. It provides insights into what went wrong, why it went wrong, and what can be done differently in the future.

This mindset shift encourages you to ask constructive questions like:

What specific factors led to this outcome?
What can I learn from this experience?
How can I adjust my approach for better results next time?

For example, if you fail to secure a job you wanted, it's not a sign that you're unworthy. It's an opportunity to evaluate your preparation, interview performance, or whether the job truly aligned with your skills and goals. Each failed attempt brings you closer to landing the right role.

Stories of Failure Leading to Success

History is filled with examples of people who turned failure into their greatest asset.

Let's take a closer look at a few inspiring stories:

Thomas Edison
Edison famously said, "I have not failed. I've just found 10,000 ways that won't work." His relentless experimentation eventually led to the invention of the light bulb, revolutionizing the world.

Imagine if Edison had given up after his first few failed attempts. His perseverance and ability to see each failure as valuable feedback were the keys to his success.

J.K. Rowling

Before Harry Potter became a global phenomenon, Rowling faced rejection from 12 publishers. She was struggling financially and raising a child as a single mother. Instead of letting the rejections defeat her, she used them to refine her manuscript and storytelling. Her eventual success is a testament to her resilience.

Walt Disney

Early in his career, Disney was fired from a newspaper job for "lacking creativity." He also faced bankruptcy several times before creating the iconic Disney brand. Each failure taught him important lessons about the entertainment industry, financial management, and perseverance.

These stories show that failure is not an endpoint but a vital part of the journey to success. Every setback carries within it the seeds of growth and innovation.

The Science of Learning from Failure

Psychologists and neuroscientists have studied the role of failure in human learning. Research shows that our brains are wired to adapt when we encounter mistakes. When you fail at something, your brain processes the error and seeks alternative strategies. This is how you grow and improve.

For example, when you learn a new skill—be it cooking, playing an instrument, or coding—mistakes are inevitable. Each mistake helps your brain refine its understanding and build new neural pathways.

By practicing and adjusting, you eventually master the skill.

This scientific insight underscores the importance of embracing failure as a natural and necessary part of learning.

Strategies to Reframe Failure

To effectively view failure as feedback, adopt the following strategies:

Detach Emotion from Failure

It's normal to feel disappointed, but don't let emotions cloud your judgment. Take a step back and objectively analyze the situation. Treat failure like a puzzle to solve rather than a verdict on your abilities.

Adopt a Growth Mindset

A growth mindset, a term popularized by psychologist Carol Dweck, emphasizes the belief that abilities can be developed through effort and learning. People with this mindset see challenges and failures as opportunities to grow, not as threats to their identity.

Celebrate the Effort, Not Just the Outcome

Recognize that effort itself is a form of progress. Even if you don't achieve your goal immediately, the skills, knowledge, and resilience you gain along the way are invaluable.

Seek Constructive Feedback

Ask others for their perspective on what went wrong and how you can improve. Constructive feedback from trusted sources can provide clarity and actionable steps for moving forward.

Set Realistic Expectations

Unrealistic goals can set you up for unnecessary disappointment. Break larger goals into smaller, achievable milestones. This approach not only reduces the likelihood of failure but also makes it easier to bounce back if things don't go as planned.

Visualize Your Comeback

Spend time visualizing how you'll respond to setbacks with courage and determination. This mental rehearsal can make it easier to stay positive and proactive when challenges arise.

Failure Builds Resilience

Resilience is the ability to recover from adversity. Each failure you overcome strengthens your resilience, making you better equipped to handle future challenges. Resilience is like a muscle—you build it by facing and overcoming difficulties.

Consider athletes, for instance. They don't achieve greatness without enduring countless losses, injuries, and moments of doubt. What sets them apart is their ability to rise each time they fall, using their setbacks to fuel their determination.

You, too, can cultivate resilience by embracing failure as a natural and necessary part of the journey.

Inspiring Action

As you finish reading this chapter, take a moment to reflect on your past failures. Write them down, along with the lessons they taught you. Acknowledge the strength you gained from overcoming them. This simple exercise can help you reframe failure in a positive light.

Next, think about a goal you've been hesitant to pursue due to fear of failure. Challenge yourself to take the first step toward it. Remember, every great achievement begins with a willingness to try, fail, and try again.

Failure is not your enemy; it's your greatest ally in the pursuit of growth and success. By viewing failure as feedback, you empower yourself to learn, adapt, and persevere. Each setback becomes a stepping stone, guiding you toward your goals.

Remember, the road to success is rarely a straight line. It's a winding path filled with detours, challenges, and moments of doubt. But with the right mindset, every failure becomes an opportunity to learn, grow, and ultimately triumph.

Embrace failure, and you'll discover that it's not the end of the road—it's just the beginning of a new and better journey.

A Failure Analysis Worksheet

Failure is an inevitable part of life, and how we respond to it shapes our personal and financial success. While many people fear failure, it is a powerful teacher when approached with the right mindset.

To turn failure into a stepping stone for success, a structured approach is essential. A failure analysis worksheet can help you reflect, learn, and strategize for the future.

Let's break this down into three key sections:

What happened? What can I learn? How do I move forward?

1. What Happened?

The first step in analyzing failure is understanding the situation clearly. It's tempting to gloss over unpleasant details, but an honest review is crucial for growth.

Key Questions to Ask:

What specific goal or outcome was I trying to achieve?
What actions did I take to reach this goal?
What were the external and internal factors influencing the situation?
What was the result, and how did it differ from my expectations?

Tips for Effective Reflection:

Be honest, not critical: This is a fact-finding mission, not a blame game. Avoid self-judgment.

Avoid emotional language: Stick to objective descriptions, such as, "I missed the deadline because I underestimated the time required," instead of, "I failed because I'm terrible at time management."

Identify patterns: If this is not your first failure in a particular area, note recurring themes.

For instance, do deadlines consistently trip you up? Is communication with others a sticking point?

Example: Imagine you invested in a business idea, and it didn't yield profits.

Goal: Launch a successful e-commerce store.

Actions Taken: Purchased inventory, designed a website, ran social media ads.

External Factors: Competitor pricing was lower; customer interest in the product niche was limited.

Internal Factors: Limited research into target audience preferences; overconfidence in ad effectiveness.

Result: Lost $5,000 in six months without significant sales.

2. What Can I Learn?

Every failure contains valuable lessons. This step involves extracting those lessons to prevent similar mistakes in the future. It's about turning the failure into wisdom.

Key Questions to Ask:

What mistakes did I make? Were they due to lack of knowledge, skill, or planning?
Which external factors were beyond my control, and how could I mitigate their impact next time?
What strengths did I demonstrate, even in failure? (For instance, resilience, creativity, or problem-solving.)
How can I reframe this failure as an opportunity for growth?

Tips for Gaining Insights:

Focus on improvement: Shift from "Why did this happen to me?" to "What can this teach me?"

Challenge assumptions: Perhaps you assumed a particular strategy was foolproof. Ask whether this assumption was valid and how you can test ideas more rigorously next time.

Seek feedback: Sometimes, outside perspectives can reveal blind spots. A mentor, friend, or professional in your field may offer insights you hadn't considered.

Example Lessons from the Business Failure

Lack of market research was a key mistake. I should have conducted surveys to understand demand for the product before investing in inventory.

My advertising strategy relied too heavily on social media ads, which didn't reach the right audience. Testing different marketing channels is critical.

Resilience was a strength. Despite setbacks, I stayed committed to the project and gained experience in website design and online sales.

3. How Do I Move Forward?

This final section focuses on creating actionable steps for the future. Reflecting and learning are valuable only if they lead to change. Here's where you craft your recovery and growth plan.

Key Questions to Ask:

What immediate steps can I take to address any damage caused by the failure?
What long-term strategies will I implement to avoid similar pitfalls?
How can I use this experience to build a stronger foundation for future success?
Are there new skills, resources, or networks I need to invest in?

Tips for Crafting an Action Plan:

Set SMART Goals: Specific, Measurable, Achievable, Relevant, and Time-bound objectives help translate insights into progress. Prioritize growth areas: Focus on the most critical skills or habits that will yield the greatest improvement. Celebrate small wins: Building confidence after a failure involves acknowledging progress, no matter how minor.

Example Action Plan:

Immediate Steps:
Sell leftover inventory at a discounted price to recover some costs.
Reach out to a business mentor for advice on pivoting strategies.

Long-term Strategies:
Conduct market research for 6 weeks before launching any new product. Experiment with at least 3 advertising platforms, including influencer partnerships, email campaigns, and SEO.
Take an online course on digital marketing by the end of the quarter.

Growth Goals:
Develop a growth mindset by reading one book on entrepreneurship each month.
Network with five successful e-commerce entrepreneurs within the next six months.

Using the Worksheet Effectively

A failure analysis worksheet is only as effective as your willingness to engage with it.

Here are some tips to make the most of it:

Dedicate time regularly: Failure isn't always dramatic or obvious. Small setbacks also deserve analysis. Spend an hour each week reflecting on what went well and what didn't.

Adapt the process: If a three-section format feels overwhelming, simplify it. Even jotting down brief answers to the key questions can help you make progress.

Review periodically: Look back at past worksheets to track your growth over time. You'll notice patterns in your mistakes and strengths, helping you refine your approach further.

Turning Failure into Strength

Failure doesn't define you; your response to it does. By using a failure analysis worksheet, you transform what seems like a setback into a setup for success. Every failed investment, poor decision, or missed opportunity is a chance to learn something that will guide you closer to financial independence and life satisfaction.

Adopting this habit not only helps you recover from failures but also strengthens your ability to navigate future challenges. The next time you face a stumble, remember: what feels like the end of the road is often just a bend in the journey toward your Rich Dad mindset.

Chapter 9: Teaching the Next Generation

One of the most profound responsibilities we carry as individuals is the duty to educate and empower the next generation. Whether they are our children, students, or members of our community, the lessons we impart can shape their futures in meaningful and lasting ways.

In the context of financial well-being and life success, teaching the next generation becomes even more critical, as it equips them with tools to navigate the challenges of an ever-changing world.

Why Teaching the Next Generation Matters

The world today is vastly different from the one many of us grew up in. With rapid technological advancements, shifting economic landscapes, and increasing financial complexities, the skills needed to thrive are constantly evolving.

While traditional education often focuses on academics, there is a growing gap when it comes to teaching practical, life-oriented skills like financial literacy, decision-making, and emotional resilience.

Teaching the next generation isn't just about giving them knowledge; it's about fostering independence, critical thinking, and the confidence to make informed choices.

When young people are equipped with these skills early on, they are better prepared to face challenges, seize opportunities, and avoid common pitfalls.

The Role of Financial Literacy

Financial literacy is one of the most valuable gifts we can give to the next generation. Yet, it is often overlooked in formal education systems.

Concepts like budgeting, saving, investing, and understanding debt are rarely taught in schools, leaving young people to learn them through trial and error.

Unfortunately, this lack of education can lead to costly mistakes that take years to recover from.

By teaching financial literacy at an early age, we can help the next generation build strong financial foundations. This includes understanding how money works, recognizing the importance of delayed gratification, and appreciating the value of setting and achieving financial goals. A child who learns to save a portion of their allowance, for instance, is more likely to develop a habit of saving as an adult.

Practical Ways to Teach Financial Skills

Start with Basics: Begin with simple concepts like distinguishing between needs and wants. Use real-life examples to illustrate the difference, such as explaining why buying groceries is a need while purchasing a new video game might be a want.

Create Opportunities for Hands-On Learning: Allow children to manage small amounts of money through allowances or chores. Encourage them to divide their money into categories like saving, spending, and giving, which can instill a balanced approach to money management.

Teach Through Stories and Games: Children often respond well to stories and interactive activities.

Use books, board games, or apps designed to teach financial skills in a fun and engaging way.

Lead by Example: Children learn by observing the adults around them. Demonstrate responsible financial behavior by budgeting, saving, and making thoughtful spending choices. Share your reasoning behind these decisions to provide context.

Introduce Real-World Concepts Gradually: As they grow older, introduce more complex topics like credit, interest rates, and investments. This can be done through conversations, educational videos, or even guided visits to a bank.

Encourage Entrepreneurship: Supporting young people in starting small business ventures, like a lemonade stand or online craft store, can teach them valuable lessons about earning, customer service, and the value of hard work.

Beyond Money: Life Lessons That Matter

While financial education is crucial, teaching the next generation goes beyond dollars and cents. It's about equipping them with a mindset that embraces lifelong learning, adaptability, and emotional intelligence.

Here are some additional lessons to consider:

The Power of Resilience: Life is full of ups and downs, and failure is often a stepping stone to success. Teach children to view setbacks as opportunities for growth and encourage them to develop a problem-solving mindset.

The Importance of Gratitude and Giving Back: Cultivate a sense of gratitude by encouraging young people to recognize and appreciate what they have. At the same time, teach them the value of giving back to others, whether through time, money, or acts of kindness.

Effective Communication Skills: Strong communication skills are essential for success in every area of life. Help children learn to express themselves clearly, listen actively, and resolve conflicts constructively.

Critical Thinking and Decision-Making: Teach young people to evaluate situations critically, weigh their options, and make informed decisions. This can involve simple exercises like discussing the pros and cons of a choice or encouraging them to ask questions and seek information.

Time Management and Goal Setting: Help children understand the importance of managing their time wisely and setting achievable goals. Teach them to break larger tasks into smaller, manageable steps and celebrate their progress along the way.

Creating a Legacy of Learning

Teaching the next generation is not a one-time effort; it's an ongoing process that requires patience, creativity, and adaptability. It's about planting seeds that may take years to grow but will eventually bear fruit in the form of confident, capable, and compassionate individuals.

One way to ensure this legacy is to create a culture of learning within families and communities. This could involve regular family discussions about money, organizing workshops on life skills, or mentoring young people in your neighborhood. Collaboration with schools and organizations can also amplify these efforts, ensuring that essential life skills are accessible to all.

Overcoming Challenges

Teaching the next generation can come with its challenges. Young people may not always be receptive, especially when topics seem abstract or unrelated to their current lives. To overcome this, focus on making lessons relevant and relatable. Connect concepts to their interests and goals, and use examples from their daily experiences to drive points home.

Additionally, be prepared to address your own gaps in knowledge. Teaching is as much about learning as it is about imparting information. If you're unsure about a topic, take the opportunity to learn together with the young person you're guiding.

A Vision for the Future

Imagine a future where every child grows up with the tools to manage their finances, make sound decisions, and lead fulfilling lives. Imagine a generation that values hard work, integrity, and the power of community. This vision is within our reach if we commit to teaching the next generation with intention and purpose.

Ultimately, teaching the next generation is about more than preparing them for the future; it's about empowering them to shape it. By investing in their growth, we create a ripple effect that extends far beyond our own lifetimes, ensuring a brighter, more prosperous world for all.

A Father's Treasure Chest

Lessons in Wealth Beyond Money

The warm, amber glow of a setting sun streamed through the window as ten-year-old Liam sat cross-legged on the living room floor. His father, Mr. Riley, a man with a weathered face and kind eyes, pulled a small, mysterious wooden chest from the top shelf of a closet. Liam's eyes widened with curiosity.

"Is it full of gold coins, Dad?" he asked eagerly.
Mr. Riley chuckled. "Not exactly, but it's worth more than gold. This, my boy, is the Treasure Chest of Lessons. Inside are the keys to understanding what it means to be rich."
Liam frowned. "But we're not rich. I heard you tell Mom last week that we can't afford a new car."

Make Poor Dad Rich Dad

Mr. Riley smiled, his voice calm and measured. "We may not have a new car, but richness isn't always about the money in your pocket. Let me show you." He opened the chest, revealing an assortment of objects: a rusty hammer, a small bundle of notes, a faded photograph, and a single shiny coin.

Liam leaned in, puzzled but intrigued. "What does all this mean?"

Lesson One: The Hammer of Hard Work

Picking up the hammer, Mr. Riley placed it gently in his son's hands. "This hammer belonged to your grandpa. He worked as a carpenter, building homes for other families. Do you know what he told me when I was your age?"
Liam shook his head.
"He said, 'A hammer isn't just a tool to build things. It's a reminder that hard work shapes not just wood, but your life, too. Wealth doesn't grow from laziness. It grows when you work hard and do your best.'"
Liam nodded thoughtfully. "So... if I work hard in school, I can earn a lot of money later?"
Mr. Riley's face grew serious, but his tone remained kind. "It's not just about money, Liam. Hard work gives you something more important—skills and character. With those, the money will come, and you'll be ready to use it wisely."

Lesson Two: The Power of Saving

Mr. Riley then pulled out the bundle of notes. Each one had numbers scrawled in pencil.
"These are the amounts I saved from my allowance when I was your age," he explained. "Your grandma taught me to always save a part of what I earned. Even when I wanted to spend it all on candy or toys, she'd remind me, 'Little streams fill big rivers.'"
Liam picked up the bundle, inspecting it with awe. "So you saved all this for years?"

"Not just saved," his father replied. "I planned. I saved enough to buy my first bicycle, and later, my first set of tools. Saving is like planting seeds. It takes time to grow, but when it does, you'll have something valuable."

"What are you saving for now?" Liam asked, curious.
"For you and your sister's future," Mr. Riley said with a smile. "And maybe, one day, for a new car."

Lesson Three: The Value of Relationships

Next, Mr. Riley held up the faded photograph. It showed a younger version of himself with his parents and two siblings. They were standing in front of a small, modest house, beaming at the camera.

"See this?" Mr. Riley said, pointing to the photo. "This was taken when I was about your age. We didn't have much, but we had each other. My dad used to say, 'A rich man isn't the one with the most money. He's the one with the strongest family and friends.'"

Liam looked up, puzzled. "But how does that make you rich?"
"Because, Liam, when times get tough—and they will—your relationships are what will help you stand back up. Your family, your friends, the people who love and support you—they're your real wealth. They make life worth living."

Liam smiled, glancing at the photograph again. "I think I get it now."

Lesson Four: The One Shiny Coin

Finally, Mr. Riley handed Liam the shiny coin. It wasn't special, just a plain silver dollar, but it gleamed brightly under the light. "This coin is a reminder of what money truly is," Mr. Riley explained. "It's a tool. It can buy things, yes, but it doesn't define who you are. Never let money control your decisions or your happiness."

"But if we don't have enough, doesn't that mean we can't be happy?" Liam asked, his voice tinged with worry.

"That's the trick, my boy," his father said, tapping the coin lightly on the table. "Happiness comes from living wisely with what you have and working toward what you want. It's not about the amount; it's about how you use it. This coin can buy candy today, or it can grow into something bigger tomorrow if you save it."

Liam turned the coin over in his hand, a spark of understanding lighting up his face.

Putting the Lessons Together

As they packed the items back into the chest, Mr. Riley turned to Liam with a warm expression.

"Do you know why I'm sharing these lessons with you?"
Liam nodded. "Because you want me to be rich someday?"
"Not just rich in money," Mr. Riley replied. "I want you to be rich in wisdom, kindness, and resilience. Money is just one piece of the puzzle. If you have the right mindset, you'll find that wealth follows naturally."

Liam hugged his dad tightly, a mix of gratitude and determination filling his heart. "I'll try my best, Dad. I promise."

Years Later

Decades later, Liam found himself standing in his own living room, his young daughter sitting cross-legged on the floor before him. In his hands was the same wooden chest, now worn but still full of its treasures.

"This," Liam said, his voice steady with emotion, "is the Treasure Chest of Lessons. It's something my dad gave me when I was your age. Let me show you what's inside."

As he opened the chest, Liam felt a surge of warmth and pride. He wasn't just passing on objects; he was passing on a legacy—a legacy of values, hard work, and love that had made him rich in ways money could never buy.

And as his daughter leaned in with wide, curious eyes, Liam knew that the lessons of the treasure chest would continue to shape generations to come.

Legacy of Financial Literacy

Have you ever stopped to think about the legacy you are building? Not just the name or memories you'll leave behind but the ripple effect of your financial decisions.

Imagine the power of shaping not just your future but also that of your children, grandchildren, and even those you'll never meet.

The Ripple Effect of Financial Literacy

Financial literacy is more than knowing how to save, invest, or budget—it's a mindset. It's about understanding how money works and using that knowledge to create stability, growth, and opportunities.

Consider the ripple effect: when you become financially literate, your actions influence those around you. You inspire others to think critically about money, take ownership of their financial lives, and break free from cycles of debt or dependency.

When one person decides to learn and teach financial literacy, they plant a seed. That seed can grow into a family culture of smart decision-making, independence, and resilience.

By empowering yourself, you're creating ripples that can touch your family, friends, and even your community.

Thinking Beyond Today is Building a Legacy

It's easy to get caught up in the here and now. Bills need paying, groceries need buying, and life is often a whirlwind of demands. But have you ever thought about the legacy your financial habits are creating?

Each choice you make—good or bad—sets an example. If you're careless with money, you may unintentionally pass that habit to your children. But if you're diligent, informed, and intentional, you pave the way for future generations to build on your successes.

Imagine a family tree where each generation is wealthier—not just financially but also in knowledge and skills. This isn't about being rich for the sake of riches.

It's about having the freedom to pursue dreams, take risks, and help others. That's the kind of legacy worth building.

Start Where You Are

Many people shy away from financial literacy because they feel they're too far behind. Maybe you grew up in a household where money was tight, or perhaps you've made mistakes in the past.

But here's the truth: it's never too late to start. Small, consistent steps can lead to profound changes over time.

Start by assessing where you are. What's your income, your expenses, your debt? Knowledge is power, and understanding your current financial picture is the first step to improvement.

From there, set goals—short-term, like paying off a credit card, and long-term, like buying a home or saving for retirement. Every journey starts with a single step, and each step forward builds momentum.

As you grow in your financial literacy, don't keep your knowledge to yourself. Share it! Talk openly with your family about budgeting, saving, and investing. Normalize discussions about money—it shouldn't be a taboo topic. Teach your children from a young age how to handle money wisely. Show them that every dollar is a choice: spend it, save it, or grow it.

When you pass down financial wisdom, you're giving the next generation a head start. They won't have to learn through trial and error because you've already laid a foundation for them. The knowledge you share today could save them years of struggle and open doors you never imagined.

The Emotional Side of Financial Literacy

Money is deeply emotional. For many, it's tied to feelings of security, self-worth, or even shame. Financial literacy isn't just about spreadsheets—it's about changing your relationship with money.

When you take control of your finances, you gain confidence. You feel empowered rather than fearful. And when you teach this mindset to your children or community, you're giving them a priceless gift: the ability to approach money with clarity and courage, rather than anxiety.

Breaking the Cycle

If you come from a background where money was always a struggle, you know how hard it can be to break the cycle. But breaking it is possible—and it starts with you. It's about taking the lessons of hardship and turning them into stepping stones for success.

Think about the stories of families who went from struggling to thriving in just a generation. Those transformations didn't happen by chance. They happened because someone decided to change the narrative. Someone chose to learn, to grow, and to teach. You can be that someone.

The Bigger Picture: Community Impact

Financial literacy isn't just about individual or family success—it's about strengthening entire communities. When more people are financially literate, communities become more stable and prosperous. There's less reliance on predatory lending, fewer financial emergencies, and more opportunities for local businesses and initiatives.

Imagine the impact if every household in a neighborhood prioritized financial education. The ripple effects would be extraordinary: higher homeownership rates, better educational opportunities for children, and a stronger sense of collective progress. By focusing on your own financial literacy, you're contributing to a broader movement of empowerment and growth.

Legacy Is More Than Money

While financial stability is an essential part of a legacy, it's not the only piece. The values you instill, the lessons you teach, and the example you set are just as important. Legacy is about the total impact you leave behind—not just the wealth, but the wisdom.

Teach integrity, hard work, and generosity alongside budgeting and investing. Show that success isn't just about accumulating wealth but about using it to make a difference. These values will resonate long after you're gone, shaping not just your descendants but also the world they inhabit.

A Call to Action

You have the power to change your financial story—and by doing so, you can inspire others to change theirs. Start small, think big, and always keep the ripple effect in mind.
Your efforts today can create waves of positive change that extend far beyond your lifetime.

Take the first step. Learn, teach, and act. The legacy you build will be one of empowerment, resilience, and endless possibility. And that's a legacy worth striving for.

Age-Specific Lesson Plans for Kids and Teens

Financial Lessons for Young Kids (Ages 5-8)

At this age, children are naturally curious and love to explore. Teaching them about money can be fun, engaging, and simple.

Understanding Money Basics

Introduce the concept of money through play. Use toy cash registers, pretend currencies, or simple board games like Monopoly Junior. Explain the value of coins and notes, and help them distinguish between needs (food, shelter) and wants (toys, candies).

Saving for a Goal

Start with a clear goal they can relate to, like saving for a favorite toy. Provide a piggy bank or jar and encourage them to put in any small earnings, such as an allowance or birthday money. Celebrate their progress by counting the savings together periodically.

Earning Money

Introduce the idea that money is earned. Assign simple chores like watering plants or sorting laundry, and reward them with small amounts of money. This helps them connect effort with income.

Financial Lessons for Pre-Teens (Ages 9-12)

As children grow, their ability to grasp more complex concepts improves. Use this stage to teach them practical financial skills.

Budgeting Basics

Teach them how to create a basic budget. For example, if they receive a $10 allowance, break it down into categories: savings (40%), spending (40%), and giving (20%). Encourage them to track their spending to see where their money goes.

The Power of Saving

Introduce compound interest in simple terms. Use examples like, "If you save $1 today and add $1 every week, how much will you have in a year?" Show how small, consistent savings can grow over time.

Comparing Prices

Involve them in grocery shopping or online browsing. Teach them to compare prices and understand the value of money. For instance, explain why buying a bulk pack of snacks may save money in the long run compared to smaller packages.

Financial Lessons for Teens (Ages 13-18)

Teenagers are on the brink of independence. Teaching them advanced financial skills prepares them for real-world challenges.

Managing a Bank Account

Open a joint savings account where they can deposit their earnings from part-time jobs, allowances, or gifts. Teach them how to use online banking apps and monitor transactions responsibly.

Credit Awareness

Explain how credit cards work and the dangers of debt. Use hypothetical examples to show how interest accumulates if payments are not made on time.

Understanding Needs vs. Wants

As teens face peer pressure and advertisements, teach them how to prioritize spending. For example, ask them to list items they wish to buy and categorize them as "essential" or "optional." Discuss the choices together.

Part-Time Jobs and Taxes

Encourage them to take up part-time jobs, such as babysitting, tutoring, or freelancing. Use their first paycheck as a teaching moment to explain income taxes and why deductions occur.

A Family Budgeting Activity

Creating a family budgeting activity is an excellent way to instill financial responsibility while fostering teamwork and understanding among family members.

Here's a step-by-step guide to a fun and educational budgeting exercise:

Step 1: Define the Goal

Start by deciding what the family budget aims to achieve. It could be saving for a vacation, reducing monthly expenses, or simply understanding where the money goes.

For example, the goal might be to save $500 for a weekend trip.

Step 2: Gather Information

Sit down as a family and list all income sources. This could include salaries, side gigs, and even allowances.

Then, list all monthly expenses, such as rent, groceries, utilities, transportation, entertainment, and savings.

Step 3: Create a Budget Template

On a large sheet of paper or a shared digital document, divide the family's expenses into categories like:

Essentials: Rent/mortgage, utilities, groceries, transportation.

Savings: Emergency fund, education fund, or specific goals like vacations.

Discretionary Spending: Dining out, entertainment, shopping.

Allocate percentages to each category. For instance, 50% for essentials, 20% for savings, and 30% for discretionary spending.

Step 4: Make It Interactive

Assign roles to each family member:

Income Tracker: Keeps a record of all money coming in.

Expense Manager: Tracks spending and ensures it aligns with the budget.

Savings Monitor: Checks progress toward savings goals.

Auditor: Reviews the budget weekly to suggest adjustments.

This way, everyone feels involved and learns financial skills.

Step 5: Track and Adjust

Each week, gather to review the budget. Celebrate successes, like staying within limits or hitting savings targets.

If there's overspending, brainstorm ways to cut back.

For example, instead of dining out, plan a family cooking night.

Step 6: Add a Fun Challenge

Turn budgeting into a friendly competition.

For example:

Challenge each family member to find one way to save money each week.

Reward the person with the most creative idea (e.g., movie night at home instead of a theater trip).

Step 7: Reflect and Learn

At the end of the budgeting period, discuss what worked and what didn't. Did the family achieve the goal? What habits can be continued moving forward? This reflection encourages everyone to see budgeting as a tool for achieving dreams rather than a restriction.

Why These Lessons Matter

By incorporating age-specific lessons and engaging the whole family in budgeting, will empowers you to build strong financial foundations. Teaching kids and teens about money equips them with life-long skills, while family activities reinforce the importance of teamwork and financial awareness.

Chapter 10: The Rich Dad Mindset for Life

The "Rich Dad Mindset" is a way of thinking and approaching life that empowers individuals to create wealth, maintain it, and use it to improve their lives and the lives of others. This mindset isn't just about accumulating money—it's about cultivating habits, values, and perspectives that lead to financial freedom and personal fulfillment. Adopting this mindset can transform not only your bank account but also your approach to challenges, relationships, and opportunities.

1. Embracing Responsibility for Your Financial Future

The foundation of the Rich Dad mindset is taking full responsibility for your financial decisions and outcomes. People with this mindset understand that no one else—whether it's the government, employers, or even family—will secure their financial future. They recognize that the power to change their circumstances lies in their hands.

This attitude pushes them to educate themselves about finances, plan strategically, and take calculated risks. Instead of blaming external factors for setbacks, they view challenges as opportunities to learn and grow.

2. The Power of Financial Education

A Rich Dad knows that financial education is the key to unlocking wealth. While traditional schooling often focuses on academic subjects, financial education involves understanding concepts like investments, savings, budgeting, taxes, and cash flow.

With the right knowledge, Rich Daddies can distinguish between assets and liabilities. They prioritize acquiring assets—things that put money in their pockets—and avoid unnecessary liabilities that drain their resources.

This knowledge allows them to make informed decisions, seize opportunities, and avoid common financial pitfalls.

3. Thinking Long-Term, Not Short-Term

Many people get stuck in a cycle of living paycheck to paycheck, focusing only on immediate needs. A Rich Daddy breaks out of this trap by thinking long-term.

They set clear financial goals and work steadily towards them, even if the journey requires patience and discipline.

This long-term mindset also applies to their investments. Rather than chasing quick profits, they focus on strategies that yield sustainable returns over time.

This approach builds a solid financial foundation, ensuring security and growth for years to come.

4. Turning Challenges into Opportunities

Life is full of challenges, but the Rich Dad mindset thrives on seeing problems as opportunities in disguise. Whether it's a market downturn or a personal financial setback, those with this mindset look for ways to learn, adapt, and capitalize on the situation.

For instance, during economic recessions, many Rich Daddies find opportunities to invest in undervalued assets, knowing these will likely increase in value when the economy recovers.

Their optimism and resourcefulness set them apart, allowing them to turn adversity into advantage.

5. The Value of Networking and Relationships

Rich Daddies understand that wealth isn't just about money—it's also about people. Building meaningful relationships with others opens doors to opportunities, collaborations, and knowledge that can accelerate financial success.

They surround themselves with like-minded individuals who inspire and challenge them to grow. They also believe in the principle of giving value before expecting anything in return. By helping others succeed, they create a network of trust and reciprocity, which becomes invaluable in their financial journey.

6. Mastering Emotional Discipline

Money can evoke strong emotions, from fear and greed to guilt and envy. Rich Daddies master their emotions, ensuring that these feelings don't dictate their financial decisions. Instead of panicking during a market downturn, they stay calm and make rational choices based on research and strategy.

This emotional discipline also extends to their spending habits. They resist the temptation to splurge on things that don't align with their financial goals, prioritizing investments that will yield long-term benefits over instant gratification.

7. The Importance of Multiple Income Streams

Relying on a single source of income is risky, as job security can never be guaranteed. Rich Daddies mitigate this risk by building multiple streams of income.

These can include investments in stocks, real estate, businesses, or passive income-generating opportunities like royalties or dividends.

Diversifying income streams not only provides financial stability but also accelerates wealth-building. It allows them to weather financial storms without significant disruption to their lifestyle.

8. Continuous Learning and Adaptability

The world of finance and business is ever-changing, and Rich Daddies stay ahead by continuously learning and adapting. They read books, attend seminars, follow industry trends, and seek advice from experts to remain informed.

This commitment to lifelong learning ensures they're always prepared for new opportunities. It also enables them to pivot when circumstances change, whether it's adapting to technological advancements or responding to shifts in the global economy.

9. The Role of Generosity and Legacy

For Rich Daddies, wealth is not just about personal gain—it's also about making a positive impact. They see money as a tool to create opportunities, support their families, and contribute to their communities. Generosity is a core principle, whether it's through charitable donations, mentoring, or creating jobs.

They also think about the legacy they want to leave behind. This means teaching their children financial literacy, creating generational wealth, and inspiring others to adopt a Rich Dad mindset.

10. Balancing Wealth and Well-Being

A true Rich Dad understands that wealth means little without health and happiness. They strive for a balanced life, ensuring that their pursuit of financial success doesn't come at the expense of their physical health, mental well-being, or personal relationships.

They prioritize self-care, invest in experiences that bring joy, and spend quality time with loved ones. This holistic approach ensures they enjoy the fruits of their labor while staying grounded and fulfilled.

11. Action-Oriented and Solution-Focused

Dreaming of wealth is one thing, but achieving it requires action. Rich Daddies are doers—they set plans in motion and take consistent steps toward their goals.

They don't wait for the "perfect" moment to act because they understand that progress is more important than perfection.

They also remain solution-focused. Instead of dwelling on problems, they channel their energy into finding creative and practical solutions, ensuring they remain proactive in their financial journey.

12. The Mindset of Abundance

Finally, the Rich Dad mindset is rooted in abundance. This means believing that wealth and opportunities are not finite but available to anyone willing to work for them.

This belief eliminates feelings of jealousy or competition and fosters collaboration and generosity.

The abundance mindset also encourages gratitude. Rich Daddies take time to appreciate their progress and recognize the blessings in their lives, which motivates them to keep striving while maintaining a positive outlook.

The Rich Dad mindset isn't reserved for a select few—it's accessible to anyone willing to adopt its principles and put them into practice. By embracing responsibility, focusing on financial education, thinking long-term, and nurturing relationships, anyone can build wealth and live a fulfilling life.

This mindset is about more than just making money; it's about creating a life of purpose, balance, and contribution. Start today, and with persistence, you too can cultivate the Rich Dad mindset and transform your financial future.

Adapting and Thriving Financially Lessons from Inspiring Figures

The world of finance is ever-changing, often compared to a river that never flows the same way twice. From turbulent economic downturns to groundbreaking innovations, those who adapt consistently demonstrate that financial resilience and growth are attainable for anyone willing to evolve. The inspiring journeys of individuals who have thrived financially, regardless of their starting points, offer invaluable lessons for aspiring achievers.

Elon Musk: Visionary Risk-Taker

Elon Musk's story is a testament to the power of adaptability and audacious vision. From co-founding PayPal to steering Tesla and SpaceX into global prominence, Musk embodies a relentless pursuit of innovation. However, his financial journey wasn't without challenges. Early in his career, Musk reinvested his earnings from PayPal's sale into Tesla and SpaceX, betting everything on industries many deemed impossible to disrupt.

When Tesla faced potential bankruptcy in its early days, Musk adapted by restructuring the company and doubling down on electric vehicles despite skepticism. Similarly, SpaceX revolutionized the aerospace industry by creating reusable rockets, a concept that was initially dismissed. Musk's story highlights a key lesson: thriving financially often requires embracing calculated risks, innovating relentlessly, and maintaining the courage to challenge conventional wisdom.

Oprah Winfrey: The Queen of Reinvention

Oprah Winfrey's rise from poverty to becoming one of the wealthiest and most influential women in the world demonstrates the power of reinvention. Born into humble beginnings, Oprah began her career as a local news anchor, but her big break came when she transformed "The Oprah Winfrey Show" into a cultural phenomenon.

Rather than resting on her success as a talk show host, Oprah ventured into production, creating Harpo Productions, and later launched OWN, the Oprah Winfrey Network. Her adaptability lies in her ability to leverage her brand across various platforms, turning her influence into a powerful financial engine.

Oprah's story reminds us that financial growth often involves evolving with changing times, embracing new platforms, and expanding your skill set.

Warren Buffett: The Sage of Consistency and Adaptation

Warren Buffett, often regarded as one of the greatest investors of all time, may not initially appear as a figure of adaptation because of his emphasis on long-term investments.

However, his success stems from his ability to adapt his strategies to changing economic climates.

For instance, during the 2008 financial crisis, Buffett capitalized on opportunities that others overlooked, investing in struggling companies like Goldman Sachs and General Electric, which later yielded significant returns.

His approach highlights a profound truth: adaptability isn't always about chasing trends but recognizing opportunities in adversity and staying patient enough to reap the rewards.

Buffett's financial journey also illustrates the importance of learning. Despite his preference for traditional industries, he recognized the transformative potential of technology and invested in Apple, which became one of Berkshire Hathaway's most profitable holdings.

His ability to adapt while staying true to his principles shows that growth often requires balancing innovation with discipline.

Sara Blakely: Turning Rejection into Opportunity

Sara Blakely, the founder of Spanx, exemplifies how resourcefulness and persistence can lead to financial success.

Starting her journey with $5,000 in savings and no prior experience in fashion, Blakely faced numerous rejections from manufacturers and investors.

However, her ability to adapt to setbacks and refine her product led to the creation of a billion-dollar shapewear brand.

Blakely's financial triumph was fueled by her willingness to listen to feedback, pivot her strategies, and learn on the go. Her story underscores the importance of resilience and creativity in adapting to challenges, proving that even small ideas, when executed with passion and flexibility, can yield massive financial returns.

Jay-Z: From Music Mogul to Business Icon

Shawn Carter, better known as Jay-Z, transitioned from a rapper to a billionaire entrepreneur by recognizing the need to diversify his income streams.

While he initially gained fame through music, Jay-Z expanded his portfolio to include investments in fashion (Rocawear), sports (Roc Nation Sports), streaming services (Tidal), and even liquor (Ace of Spades).

What sets Jay-Z apart is his ability to evolve with industry changes. In an era where music streaming disrupted traditional album sales, he launched Tidal, a platform that gave artists greater control over their royalties.

By staying ahead of trends and constantly seeking new opportunities, Jay-Z demonstrates how adaptability and foresight can lead to enduring financial success.

Indra Nooyi: Leadership in Changing Times

Indra Nooyi, the former CEO of PepsiCo, is a shining example of how adaptability at the corporate level translates to financial growth. During her tenure, Nooyi transformed PepsiCo by introducing healthier product lines and focusing on sustainability, responding to changing consumer preferences and societal pressures.

Nooyi's leadership not only increased PepsiCo's market value but also positioned the company as a forward-thinking industry leader. Her ability to anticipate trends, embrace change, and prioritize long-term value creation offers a lesson in strategic adaptability, whether managing personal finances or leading a global corporation.

Key Takeaways from These Inspiring Figures

Embrace Change: Every inspiring figure highlighted here has faced periods of uncertainty. Instead of resisting change, they embraced it as an opportunity to grow. Financial success requires being open to new ideas and willing to pivot when necessary.

Invest in Learning: Whether it's Buffett reading voraciously or Oprah exploring new ventures, continuous learning is a common thread among successful individuals. Staying informed helps you make smarter decisions and adapt to emerging trends.

Diversify Your Skills and Investments: From Jay-Z's multifaceted empire to Sara Blakely's innovative products, diversification is key. Relying on one income stream or skill can limit growth, while branching out opens up new opportunities.

Stay Resilient: Financial challenges are inevitable, but figures like Musk and Blakely prove that persistence pays off. Turning setbacks into opportunities is a defining trait of financial thrivers.

Think Long-Term: Warren Buffett and Indra Nooyi emphasize the importance of patience and strategic thinking. Quick wins may bring temporary success, but sustainable wealth requires a long-term vision.

Adaptability is the cornerstone of financial resilience and success. Whether you're starting with limited resources or managing a thriving empire, the ability to evolve with changing circumstances is a skill anyone can cultivate. By studying the journeys of these inspiring figures, you can learn how to turn challenges into stepping stones and create a financial future that is both secure and abundant. The message is clear: no matter where you begin, adaptability and a growth mindset can transform your financial story.

Reinforce the Idea of Lifelong Growth and Learning

The journey of success, whether in wealth, relationships, or personal fulfillment, is never static. Life is a continuous cycle of opportunities, challenges, and growth. The concept of lifelong growth and learning serves as the cornerstone for achieving transformation—not just financially, but holistically. This philosophy teaches us that every day brings fresh chances to build a better version of ourselves, encouraging a mindset that evolves with time and experience.

Embracing the Growth Mindset

At the heart of lifelong learning is the belief that your abilities, knowledge, and potential are not fixed. This is what psychologists call the "growth mindset," a concept that emphasizes that you can always improve through effort, learning, and persistence. Think of your mind as fertile soil. Each time you invest in your growth, whether by reading a book, learning a skill, or seeking feedback, you plant seeds.

Over time, these seeds flourish into trees of wisdom, wealth, and fulfillment.

Ask yourself daily: "What can I learn today?" This question opens the door to new possibilities and keeps your spirit curious and innovative. Lifelong learners do not wait for opportunities; they create them by staying open to new ideas, perspectives, and tools.

Small Steps Lead to Big Transformations

One powerful truth about growth is that it often happens in small, incremental steps. Imagine trying to fill a jar with drops of water. At first, it seems like nothing is happening. But over time, drop by drop, the jar fills. Similarly, each small action you take contributes to the larger picture of your personal and financial success.

Start small by setting daily affirmations like, "Every day is a new opportunity to grow my wealth," or "I am always learning and improving." These simple, positive statements rewire your thinking and remind you to keep moving forward. When faced with setbacks, remind yourself: progress, not perfection, is the goal.

Wealth as a Byproduct of Learning

Money is often a tangible measure of success, but it is not the end goal. Instead, think of wealth as a byproduct of the value you create in the world. And how do you create more value? By growing yourself. Learning a new skill, deepening your expertise, or becoming more emotionally intelligent increases the value you bring to relationships, workplaces, and communities.

For example, if you are a small business owner, learning about digital marketing could help you expand your reach. If you're an employee, developing leadership skills could lead to a promotion.

Remember: "The more I grow, the more value I can offer to others, and the more wealth I can create."

Adapting to Change

One of the greatest lessons of lifelong growth is that change is constant. The world is evolving rapidly, with technological advancements, shifting markets, and unpredictable challenges like economic downturns. Instead of fearing change, embrace it as a chance to grow.

Think about the people who thrived during major transitions in history. Whether it was adapting to the industrial revolution or leveraging the internet boom, those who succeeded were the ones who kept learning.

In today's world, staying relevant requires the same approach: keep upgrading your knowledge, skills, and strategies.

You might not know what the future holds, but you can prepare for it by staying curious. Adopt the mantra: "Change is my opportunity to grow." When you view life through this lens, challenges become stepping stones, not stumbling blocks.

Learning from Failure

Failure is often viewed as the opposite of success, but in reality, it is an essential part of growth. Every setback contains valuable lessons if you are willing to look for them. Think about a baby learning to walk. They fall countless times, but each fall teaches them how to balance better.

Similarly, every failure in your journey to wealth and success teaches you what not to do—and sometimes, what you should do differently.

Instead of fearing failure, embrace it with affirmations like: "Every failure is a lesson that brings me closer to success." The most successful people in the world failed repeatedly before they succeeded, from Thomas Edison inventing the lightbulb to entrepreneurs launching groundbreaking businesses. What sets them apart is their ability to learn and persist.

The Role of Curiosity

A curious mind is a wealthy mind. Curiosity fuels your desire to explore, ask questions, and uncover new possibilities. Think about children—they are naturally curious, always asking "Why?" or "How does this work?" As adults, we often lose this spark of curiosity because of routine or fear of looking foolish.

To reignite your curiosity, commit to learning something new every week. It could be as small as exploring a new recipe, reading an article about a topic you don't understand, or attending a seminar on personal finance. Remember: "Every new thing I learn expands my possibilities."

Investing in Yourself

One of the wisest investments you can make is in your growth. This could mean taking a course, hiring a mentor, or simply setting aside time for self-reflection and reading.

Financial literacy, in particular, is an area where investing in knowledge pays significant dividends.

If you're unsure where to start, consider this: What is one skill that could improve your income or help you manage your finances better? Dedicate time and resources to mastering it. As you grow, the opportunities to create and multiply wealth will naturally follow. Repeat to yourself: "Every dollar I invest in my growth brings me closer to financial freedom."

The Power of Consistency

Growth doesn't happen overnight. It requires consistency, discipline, and patience. Think of a plant: you can't pour water on it once and expect it to grow into a tall tree by the next morning.

Similarly, personal and financial growth requires ongoing effort.

Create daily habits that align with your goals. For example, set aside 30 minutes a day to read a book about financial strategies or practice a skill that enhances your career.

Celebrate small wins, and trust the process. As the saying goes, "Consistency compounds results."

Giving Back as Growth

Finally, true growth is not just about what you gain—it's also about what you give. Sharing your knowledge, mentoring others, or contributing to your community enhances your own learning and fulfillment.

When you help others grow, you strengthen your understanding and reinforce the habits that brought you success.

Affirm: "As I grow, I lift others along with me." Giving back is not just an act of generosity—it's a way to keep the cycle of growth alive and thriving.

Lifelong growth and learning are the foundations of a fulfilling, wealthy, and purposeful life.

By embracing a mindset of constant improvement, you not only open doors to financial success but also enrich every area of your existence.

Remember to affirm daily:

"Every day is a new opportunity to grow my wealth."
"I am always learning and improving."
"Change is my opportunity to grow."
Through these affirmations and a commitment to growth, you'll transform not only your financial situation but your entire outlook on life.

Growth is not a destination—it's a lifelong journey.

A Daily Habit Tracker for Financial Discipline

Building wealth isn't just about earning more; it's about mastering daily habits that align with financial discipline. A well-structured daily habit tracker can help you stay consistent, monitor your progress, and identify areas for improvement.

Here's how to design and implement a tracker to make financial discipline an integral part of your life.

Why Use a Daily Habit Tracker?

A daily habit tracker creates a visual record of your consistency in practicing financial habits.

It gives you:

Clarity: Identifies where your money is going and how your habits impact your financial goals.

Motivation: Seeing consistent progress can encourage you to keep going.

Accountability: Helps you stay accountable to yourself by tracking every step you take.

What to Include in Your Tracker

A well-rounded financial habit tracker should include:

Daily Expense Logging
Note every purchase you make, no matter how small.
Categorize your spending (e.g., food, entertainment, transportation) to understand your spending habits better.

Budget Check-ins
Reflect on whether you stayed within your daily budget.
If you exceeded it, note why and what adjustments are needed.

Savings Deposits
Track whether you contributed to your savings account that day.
Include a note for specific goals (e.g., emergency fund, vacation savings, or retirement).

Debt Management
Log any payments made toward debts like credit cards, loans, or mortgages.
Mark progress toward eliminating debt or reducing interest costs.

Investment Growth
Record any new investments or contributions to existing ones.
Note how much you learned about your investments that day.

Learning and Skill Development
Dedicate a section to financial education (e.g., reading a chapter of a book, listening to a podcast).
Note one takeaway or action point from your learning session.

How to Stay Consistent
Make it Simple: Use a notebook, a mobile app, or a spreadsheet that suits your style.
Set a Routine: Dedicate five to ten minutes every evening to update your tracker.
Reward Yourself: Celebrate milestones (e.g., 30 days of consistent tracking) to stay motivated.
Be Honest: Your tracker is for you, so don't fudge numbers or skip entries.
By committing to daily tracking, you'll gradually build financial discipline, reduce impulsive spending, and achieve your goals systematically.

Resources for Continued Learning

The journey to financial success requires lifelong learning. The financial world evolves rapidly, and staying updated ensures you make informed decisions. Below are some valuable resources to enrich your financial knowledge.

Books

Books are timeless resources for financial education.

Here are some must-reads:

"The Richest Man in Babylon" by George S. Clason

Offers timeless financial wisdom through engaging parables.
Learn principles like saving a portion of your income, making wise investments, and avoiding unnecessary debt.

"I Will Teach You to Be Rich" by Ramit Sethi

A practical guide to automating finances, growing wealth, and enjoying guilt-free spending.
Ideal for beginners who want actionable steps to manage money.

"The Millionaire Next Door" by Thomas J. Stanley and William D. Danko

Explores habits of financially successful people and contrasts them with high-income earners who are broke.
Teaches frugality, saving, and smart investing.

"Your Money or Your Life" by Vicki Robin and Joe Dominguez

Encourages readers to redefine their relationship with money and prioritize what truly matters.
Provides a step-by-step system to achieve financial independence.

Podcasts

Podcasts are an excellent way to learn on the go.

Here are some to consider:

"The Dave Ramsey Show"

Focuses on debt reduction, budgeting, and building wealth through simple, no-nonsense advice.
Great for anyone seeking motivation and practical strategies.

"ChooseFI"
Discusses financial independence and early retirement strategies.
Features inspiring stories from people who've achieved financial freedom.

"The Smart Passive Income Podcast" by Pat Flynn
Covers topics on building passive income streams and entrepreneurship.
Ideal for those looking to diversify income sources.

"The Investing for Beginners Podcast"
Explains investing concepts in simple terms.
Offers insights into stock market basics, portfolio management, and more.

Online Courses

Interactive courses can deepen your understanding of complex financial topics.

Check out these platforms:

Coursera
Offers courses like "Financial Markets" by Yale University and "Personal & Family Financial Planning" by the University of Florida.
Certificates can add credibility to your knowledge.

Udemy
Affordable courses covering budgeting, investing, and entrepreneurship.
Popular options include "Personal Finance Masterclass" and "Stock Market Investing for Beginners".

Khan Academy
Free lessons on personal finance topics like saving, taxes, and investing basics.
Excellent for beginners or those on a tight budget.

Skillshare
Focuses on practical skills like creating side hustles or mastering financial spreadsheets.

Apps for Ongoing Learning

Duolingo for Finance
While not literal, apps like Zogo gamify financial education. Earn rewards while learning concepts like credit, taxes, and budgeting.

Morning Brew
A free daily email newsletter breaking down financial news in a digestible format.

Bloomberg App
Provides market insights and expert opinions on financial trends.

How to Maximize These Resources

Create a Learning Schedule
Dedicate specific days to books, podcasts, or courses.
For example, listen to a podcast during your morning commute or read a book before bed.

Apply What You Learn
Implement lessons immediately, whether it's tweaking your budget or starting a small investment.

Join a Community
Engage with others through forums like Reddit's r/personalfinance or local finance meetups.
Sharing experiences and advice can amplify your learning.

By consistently using these resources, you'll stay informed, make smarter financial choices, and build lasting wealth.

From Poor Dad to Rich Dad — Your Turn

The journey from being a "Poor Dad" to a "Rich Dad" is not just about accumulating wealth; it's about redefining your relationship with money, success, and the legacy you leave behind.

This transformation is deeply personal yet universal, as it taps into a shared desire for financial security, fulfillment, and purpose.

As you stand at the threshold of your own journey, let this conclusion serve as both a reflection and a guide, reminding you that the power to change your financial story is within your grasp.

Reflecting on the Journey

Throughout this book, we've explored the core principles that differentiate the mindsets of a Poor Dad and a Rich Dad. A Poor Dad often operates from a place of fear—fear of taking risks, fear of failure, and fear of change.

On the other hand, a Rich Dad embraces opportunities, sees failures as stepping stones, and constantly adapts to life's evolving financial landscape. Understanding this fundamental contrast is the first step in shifting your mindset.

But this journey isn't solely about thinking differently; it's about acting differently. You've learned how to set personal financial goals, establish foundational habits, and draft a roadmap tailored to your unique circumstances.

These tools are your compass, helping you navigate the complexities of wealth-building with clarity and confidence.

Your Turn to Take Action

Knowledge without action is like a seed that's never planted. Now is the time to take everything you've learned and put it into practice. Start by reviewing the financial goals you've outlined in this book. Are they specific, measurable, attainable, relevant, and time-bound (SMART)? If not, refine them.

Goals give you direction, but it's your actions that will bring them to life.

Next, revisit the financial habits we discussed. Habits like budgeting, saving consistently, and investing wisely form the foundation of financial growth. These practices may seem small at first, but their cumulative impact over time can be transformative.

Think of them as the bricks in the mansion of your financial future.

Breaking the Cycle

For many, the Poor Dad mindset is a generational cycle. Perhaps you grew up in a household where financial struggles were the norm, and scarcity shaped your outlook. Breaking this cycle requires courage and persistence. It means challenging deeply ingrained beliefs, such as "Money is the root of all evil" or "Rich people are greedy." Replace these limiting beliefs with empowering ones, like "Money is a tool for freedom" and "Wealth amplifies kindness."

As you work to change your own financial story, remember that your actions have a ripple effect. By modeling healthy financial behaviors, you can inspire your children, friends, and community to do the same.

Becoming a Rich Dad is not just about personal gain—it's about creating a legacy of abundance and opportunity.

Embracing Failures as Lessons

Failure is inevitable on the path to success, but it's not the end of the road. It's a sign that you're trying, learning, and growing. Rich Daddies view failure as valuable feedback.

They analyze what went wrong, extract lessons, and adjust their strategies. This approach turns setbacks into stepping stones.

Take time to reflect on your own financial missteps. Perhaps you've overspent on credit cards, made poor investment choices, or struggled to stick to a budget.

Instead of dwelling on these mistakes, ask yourself: What can I learn from this? How can I avoid similar pitfalls in the future? Remember, every failure is an opportunity to improve.

Building Wealth Beyond Money

Being a Rich Dad is not just about having a fat bank account; it's about leading a rich life.

This means cultivating strong relationships, maintaining good health, and finding joy in your everyday experiences. Money is simply a means to enhance these aspects of life, not a goal in itself.

Take stock of your life's richness outside of financial metrics. Are you spending quality time with loved ones? Are you pursuing passions that bring you happiness? Are you giving back to your community? True wealth encompasses all these dimensions.

Staying Committed to Growth

The journey to becoming a Rich Dad is ongoing. Markets fluctuate, economies change, and personal circumstances evolve. Staying committed to growth means remaining adaptable, continuously educating yourself, and embracing lifelong learning. Consider reading more books, attending financial workshops, or seeking advice from mentors who inspire you.

It's also important to celebrate your milestones along the way. Every small victory, whether it's paying off a debt, achieving a savings goal, or successfully starting an investment, deserves recognition. Celebrating your progress keeps you motivated and reminds you of how far you've come.

Leaving a Legacy

As you transition from Poor Dad to Rich Dad, think about the legacy you want to leave behind. This isn't just about passing down wealth; it's about passing down wisdom, values, and opportunities.

Consider creating a financial plan for your family that includes teaching your children about money, setting up generational wealth systems, and supporting causes you're passionate about.

A Rich Daddy leaves the world better than he found it. He uses his resources to create positive change, inspire others, and contribute to a more equitable society. Your legacy is not just about what you accumulate but what you contribute.

The path from Poor Dad to Rich Dad is not a straight line. It's a journey filled with challenges, learning moments, and triumphs. But the most important thing to remember is that it's your journey. No one else can walk it for you, but you have the tools, knowledge, and capability to succeed.

As you close this book, take a moment to visualize the life you're working toward. See yourself as the Rich Dad you aspire to be—financially secure, emotionally fulfilled, and leaving a lasting legacy. This vision is your North Star, guiding your decisions and actions.

Now, it's your turn. Go out there, take control of your finances, and transform your life. The Rich Dad within you is waiting to be unleashed. Your future self will thank you for the steps you take today.

Recap of Key Lessons from Make Poor Dad Rich Dad

As we conclude this transformative journey, let's revisit the core lessons that will empower you to rewrite your financial story and embrace the Rich Dad mindset.

1. Mindset Matters

Poor Dad Mindset: Operates from fear, scarcity, and a reactive approach to money.

Rich Dad Mindset: Embraces abundance, opportunities, and a proactive approach to financial planning.

Lesson: Your thoughts shape your reality. Adopt a mindset that sees money as a tool for growth, not a source of stress.

2. Set SMART Financial Goals

Goals must be Specific, Measurable, Attainable, Relevant, and Time-bound (SMART).

Start with clear short-term, medium-term, and long-term goals to build a road map for your financial success.

Lesson: Clarity in your objectives is the foundation for meaningful progress.

3. Cultivate Foundational Financial Habits

Habits like budgeting, saving a percentage of your income, and living below your means create financial stability.

Automate savings and prioritize needs over wants to build a solid foundation.

Lesson: Consistency in small, positive habits leads to significant financial growth over time.

4. Master Money Management

Learn to balance earning, spending, saving, and investing. Avoid debt traps and focus on building assets that generate passive income.

Lesson: Effective money management isn't about how much you earn but how wisely you handle what you have.

5. Embrace Failures as Learning Opportunities

Financial mistakes are part of the journey; use them as tools for growth.

Reflect on what went wrong and adjust your strategies to avoid repeating the same errors.

Lesson: Every setback is a stepping stone if you learn and move forward with resilience.

6. Build Wealth Beyond Money

True wealth includes good health, meaningful relationships, and personal fulfillment.

Use financial freedom to pursue passions, spend time with loved ones, and give back to your community.

Lesson: A rich life balances financial success with emotional and social well-being.

7. Stay Committed to Continuous Learning

Financial literacy is an ongoing process. Stay informed about investments, market trends, and wealth-building strategies.

Seek out mentors, read books, and engage in financial education to refine your skills.

Lesson: Lifelong learning keeps you adaptable in an ever-changing financial landscape.

8. Leave a Lasting Legacy

Wealth is not just about money—it's about imparting wisdom, values, and opportunities to the next generation. Consider creating systems for generational wealth and teaching financial literacy to your children.

Lesson: A Rich Dad creates a legacy that inspires and empowers others.

9. Take Action

Knowledge is only powerful when paired with action. Implement what you've learned step by step. Celebrate small victories and keep moving forward, no matter how slow progress feels.

Lesson: The journey to wealth begins with the first step—your action today shapes your future.

By embodying these principles, you can transform your financial reality and become the Rich Dad of your dreams.

Steps You Can Take Immediately

Transforming from a Poor Dad to a Rich Dad starts with taking decisive action.

Here are practical steps you can implement right now to set yourself on the path to financial success:

1. Assess Your Current Financial Situation

What to Do: Take stock of your income, expenses, savings, and debts. Write everything down to get a clear picture of where you stand.

Why It Matters: You can't create a plan for improvement without knowing your starting point.

2. Set SMART Financial Goals

What to Do: Identify one short-term (e.g., save $1,000 in 3 months), one medium-term (e.g., pay off credit card debt in a year), and one long-term goal (e.g., retire comfortably with $1M in investments).

Why It Matters: Goals give your financial actions direction and purpose.

3. Create a Budget

What to Do: Allocate your income into categories: essentials, savings, investments, and discretionary spending. Use tools like budgeting apps or spreadsheets to track your progress.

Why It Matters: A budget ensures you live within your means and prioritize wealth-building.

4. Start Saving Immediately

What to Do: Open a separate savings account and automate a portion of your income to be transferred there monthly. Start with as little as 5–10% of your income.

Why It Matters: Saving consistently builds a financial cushion and enables future investments.

5. Pay Down High-Interest Debt

What to Do: List your debts and tackle those with the highest interest rates first. Use strategies like the snowball (smallest debt first) or avalanche (highest interest first) methods.

Why It Matters: Eliminating debt frees up money for savings and investments.

6. Educate Yourself on Investments

What to Do: Research investment options like stocks, bonds, real estate, or mutual funds. Start small, perhaps with a low-cost index fund, and consider speaking to a financial advisor.

Why It Matters: Investments grow your money over time and build passive income.

7. Establish a Daily Money Habit

What to Do: Spend 5–10 minutes each day reviewing your finances—track expenses, review bank statements, or read about personal finance.

Why It Matters: Regular engagement keeps you in control of your financial health.

8. Build an Emergency Fund

What to Do: Save 3–6 months' worth of living expenses in a liquid and accessible account.

Why It Matters: An emergency fund prevents financial setbacks from unexpected events like job loss or medical expenses.

9. Start a Side Hustle or Increase Income Streams

What to Do: Identify skills or passions you can monetize, such as freelancing, tutoring, or starting a small business.

Why It Matters: Additional income accelerates debt payoff, savings, and investment growth.

10. Join a Financial Accountability Group

What to Do: Surround yourself with like-minded individuals who share financial goals. Join online communities, local meetups, or create a group with friends or family.
Why It Matters: Accountability keeps you motivated and inspired.

11. Teach Your Family About Money

What to Do: Share what you've learned with your children, partner, or close friends.

Start simple conversations about saving, budgeting, and smart spending.

Why It Matters: Teaching others reinforces your own knowledge and ensures the legacy of financial literacy.

12. Commit to Continuous Learning

What to Do: Read at least one personal finance book a year, follow financial experts, and attend workshops or webinars.

Why It Matters: The financial world evolves, and staying informed helps you adapt and thrive.

Start Today, Build Tomorrow

Every small step you take today compounds into significant progress tomorrow. Don't wait for the "perfect time"—it doesn't exist.

Begin now, even if it feels overwhelming or uncertain.

Remember, the most important part of becoming a Rich Dad isn't where you are now; it's the commitment to where you're going.

Your financial transformation starts here. Take that first step and claim the future you deserve!

Continue Your Journey Toward Wealth and Success

The path to financial freedom and a rich, fulfilling life is not a sprint—it's a marathon. It's a journey filled with challenges, learning moments, and opportunities to grow into the best version of yourself.

As you stand at the starting line of this journey, remember: every step you take, no matter how small, is a victory.

Believe in Your Power to Change

Your current circumstances do not define your future. The mistakes of yesterday are lessons, not life sentences. Every successful Rich Dad started somewhere—often in places of doubt, struggle, or financial hardship.

What sets them apart is their belief in their ability to rise above and create a better tomorrow. You have that same power.

Focus on Progress, Not Perfection

Building wealth and success isn't about getting everything right all at once. It's about making consistent progress over time.

Celebrate the small wins—whether it's saving your first $100, paying off a single debt, or learning a new financial skill. These victories add up, building momentum and confidence as you move forward.

Embrace the Ups and Downs

The journey won't always be smooth. Markets will fluctuate, unexpected expenses will arise, and you may face moments of doubt. But remember: every challenge you overcome is a stepping stone to your success.

Resilience is your greatest asset. Keep going, even when the road gets tough.

Stay Inspired

Look to others who have walked this path and achieved their goals. Read their stories, learn from their experiences, and remind yourself that if they could do it, so can you.

Surround yourself with positive influences—mentors, books, and communities that encourage growth and wealth-building.

Keep Your Vision Alive

Close your eyes and imagine the life you're working toward. Picture the financial security, the opportunities you'll create for your loved ones, and the legacy you'll leave behind.

This vision is your guiding light. Whenever you feel lost or discouraged, return to it, and let it reignite your motivation.

Invest in Yourself

You are your greatest asset. The more you learn, grow, and develop, the more capable you become of achieving your goals.

Whether it's improving your financial literacy, gaining new skills, or adopting healthier habits, every investment in yourself pays dividends in the long run.

Share Your Journey

As you progress, share your story with others. Your journey can inspire and empower those around you, creating a ripple effect of positivity and change. Remember, being a Rich Dad isn't just about personal success; it's about uplifting others and leaving the world better than you found it.

Keep Moving Forward

No matter where you are on your journey, keep taking steps—one decision, one habit, one action at a time. The transformation from a Poor Dad to a Rich Dad is not about perfection; it's about persistence. With every step forward, you're rewriting your story and building a brighter future.

You've Got This

The fact that you've read this far proves your commitment to growth and change. You've already taken the first steps toward a better financial future, and that's something to be proud of. Keep that momentum alive. You're capable of more than you know, and the best is yet to come.

The Rich Dad you aspire to be is already within you. All it takes is the courage to continue, the resilience to persevere, and the determination to succeed.

Your journey toward wealth and success doesn't end here—it's just beginning. Keep going. You've got this!

Make Poor Dad Rich Dad

W J Francis

www.ingramcontent.com/pod-product-compliance
Lightning Source LLC
Chambersburg PA
CBHW071021240526
45469CB00006BD/2018